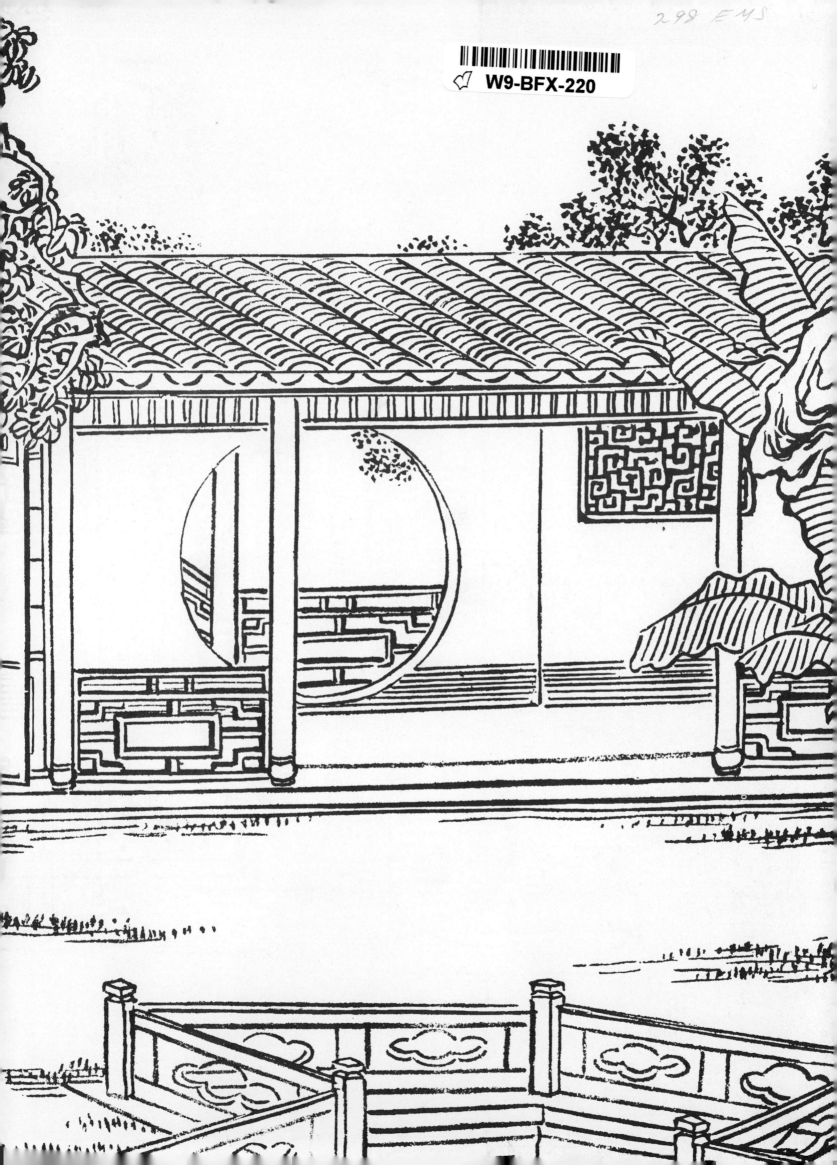

CHINESE HOUSES AND GARDENS

(yuan)   Garden

(t'ing)   House

(hua)   Picture

Choice
(ts'ui)   Collection

園庭畫萃

"A CHOICE COLLECTION OF
GARDEN AND HOUSE PICTURES"
By
HENRY INN

EDITED by SHAO CHANG LEE

CHARACTERS by CH'EN SHOU-YI

阮勉初集
李紹昌編
陳受頤題

Chinese Houses and Gardens

By

HENRY INN
Author of "Hawaiian Types"
and "Tropical Blooms"

Edited by
SHAO CHANG LEE
Author of "China, Ancient and Modern,"
"Chinese Culture Through the Moon Gate,"
"Popular Buddhism in China," etc.

BONANZA BOOKS   NEW YORK

*To Mrs. Charles Montague Cooke, Sr.,
whose life, gifts and friendship deepened
for those who shared them, appreciation
of all cultures and sensitiveness to all
beauty, this book is dedicated in grateful
and loving memory.*

Contents

Part One: Articles

Part Two: Plates

Preface

*I*N 1936 Mr. Henry Inn, a connoisseur of Chinese Art, made his tenth extensive tour of his motherland to study the designs of houses and gardens. He travelled from Canton to Peiping and from Shanghai to Wuch'ang, visiting many homes of culture and refinement built according to the traditional patterns of the art of house and garden making elaborated through centuries. It was a rare privilege granted few travellers. With the kind permission of his hosts he photographed and sketched characteristic details. On his return to Honolulu he showed the pictures and drawings to friends interested in architecture, interior decoration and landscape gardening. They all recognized their value, both as a record of a unique and significant art, and as suggestive material for Western builders and garden makers and urged their publication in book form.

In pursuance of this project the editor, who was in China that same year collecting material for a course in Chinese Art to be given at the University of Hawaii, was asked by Mr. Inn to visit the places photographed with a view to writing a chapter on Chinese symbolism expressed in building and gardening with special reference to these particular pictures. Realizing the scope and importance of the task, he enlisted the cooperation of two of his colleagues at the University of Hawaii, Dr. Ch'en Shou-Yi and Dr. Wing-Tsit Chan.

Dr. Ch'en Shou-Yi is the author of a treatise on "The Chinese Garden in Eighteenth Century England," published by the T'ien Hsia Monthly, April 1936. He gives the historical background in his chapter entitled "Chinese Houses and Gardens in Retrospect." Dr. Wing-Tsit Chan, professor of Chinese philosophy and esthetics writes on "Man and Nature in the Chinese Garden."

In addition to these chapters written especially for this book are two articles by Mr. Chuin Tung, an authority on Chinese architecture, that appeared in the October 1936 and May 1938 issues of the T'ien Hsia Monthly, reprinted with the permission of Dr. Wen Yuan-ning, editor-in-chief of the magazine. The editor has supplemented his chapter on "The Chinese Love of Home and Symbolism" with a few illustrative selections from Chinese literature, translated by himself. Mr. Edgar C. Schenck, Director of the Honolulu Academy of Arts, kindly consented to write the Introduction.

It is hoped that this book may give to its readers a sense of the fine appreciation of living beauty expressed through a subtly symbolic and decorative art that is a vital part of *the cultural inheritance of the Chinese people, and whose influence still lives, though much of its outward embodiment as shown in these pictures has been irreparably injured or completely destroyed through the ruthlessness of destructive war.*

The author and the editor wish to record their indebtedness to the many friends for their aid, interest, and encouragement, and to the Garden Club of Honolulu and the American Institute of Architects, Hawaii Chapter, for their approval and recommendation.

SHAO CHANG LEE.

University of Hawaii,
September 1, 1940.

Preface to the Second Edition

IT IS a pleasure to note that in spite of the appearance in recent years of some books on Chinese gardens there still seems to be a place for this book. The kindly reception its first edition has had at the hands of the public and the demand for its republications are an inspiration to the author and editor.

In response to demand for a second edition, the author and editor deem it wise to have the book issued in the same format as the first edition. The few typographical errors found in the previous edition have been corrected.

The author and editor again wish to acknowledge with gratitude the help they have received from friends who have given valuable suggestions and from the publishers —the University of Illinois Press, the MacMillan Company, the T'ien Hsia Monthly and the Society for Research in Chinese Architecture—who have graciously granted permission to print certain quotations from their publications that the authors of the various articles in this books have used and also acknowledged in the text.

SHAO CHANG LEE.

Michigan State College

Introduction

IT is usually a visitor who, moved by the beauty of a country, photographs or describes its scenes for those less fortunate than he and then asks a resident to write an introduction to correct any misinterpretations. For this book that normal process has been reversed. On his many visits to China, Mr. Henry Inn has photographed, measured and drawn up details of houses and gardens which he knows well and has given a westerner the privilege of writing the introduction.

The monumental architecture of any country may be discussed in accordance with its own well established principles, for this type of building is in most cases a *finished* building. But domestic architecture will inevitably suffer by such abstract analysis. An old home is an intimate thing. Its foundations are laid deep in tradition; generations of trial and error have determined its form; it houses the common denominator of human life; and into its walls are hammered the joys and sorrows, the achievements and convictions of a people. Its design reflects the texture of the individual human lives which cross its threshold and its unity is seldom that of an abstract plan, but that of a growing personality. It is like the unity of a city in which new areas develop in answer to new needs, but which, because of certain conditioning factors, keeps its individuality throughout all changes.

Mr. Inn's photographs present one part of the picture of the old Chinese home, and the writings by his distinguished collaborators another. It is fitting, therefore, that this book should be no ambitious attempt to trace influences nor an exhaustive study of the developments of architecture in any one area. The photographs illustrate houses and gardens from Canton to Peiping and from Shanghai to Hangchow and the text is concerned with subjects that range from philosophy to farming. The book thus presents an informal and intimate picture of Chinese living.

To the reader its value is twofold; the war in the Far East has given the book importance as a record of architecture and gardens which are gone forever. In addition, through it the Western reader can see and understand a relationship between house and garden which for two hundred years has influenced, in one way or another, our own home and garden planning. The Chinese garden, in which nature is not placed in the strait-jacket of a beaux-arts plan, became the rage in Europe during the 18th century. It had a tremendous influence on English architects as the so-called Anglo-Chinese gardens at Kew testify. The curious thing about this movement was that the Western mind so completely misunderstood it. The drawings and plans of Sir William Chambers show that he was impressed by the rich exotic ideals of Chinese architecture. But he used the Chinese pagoda, for example, in a contemporary English setting, as a sort of romantic escape, in the same way that architects used the Greek temple or the Gothic ruin in that sentimental century.

Later generations have been more accurate archeologically. Since the time of Chambers, scholars have studied and recorded details of the design and construction of Chinese buildings and gardens. Their concern, however, was largely with monumental architecture. Our own generation has been particularly impressed with the total effect of these buildings in their surroundings. Many beautiful collections of photographs in our libraries bear witness to the impact of the architecture of China on a picture-conscious Western world. But the flavor of the Chinese home is neither in the highly finished landscape photograph nor in the correct architectural drawing. It is rather to be found in such informal and intimate pictures as those reproduced in this book, which show for the most part, details of background that merge into a general impression, and which are seldom isolated for study.

Horace Walpole once said, "The fairest scenes that depend on themselves alone, weary when often seen. The Doric portico, the Palladian bridge, the Gothic ruin, the Chinese pagoda, that surprise the stranger soon lose their charms to their surfeited master." This disillusioned statement by the builder of that romantic pile, "Strawberry Hill," is the result of a misunderstanding of some of the essential principles of architectural style. This book of articles and photographs is a step forward in the understanding of Chinese life, without which the "Chinese pagoda" is indeed only a novelty.

EDGAR C. SCHENCK.

Part One: Articles

Chinese Houses and Gardens in Retrospect

By Ch'en Shou-Yi, Ph.D.

THE home in China, physically considered, consists of two distinct but inseparable elements—the house and the garden. Even to casual Occidental observers, houses and gardens in China have their own attractions, their own personalities which are different from their Western counterparts. If they are not superior, they are at least different. Like Chinese painting and music, like Chinese poetry and philosophy, architecture and the gardening art in China are an expression of the Chinese national genius. They are, in other words, part and parcel of China's civilization.

Speaking of Chinese civilization, it is necessary to point out that we should dismiss once for all the misconceived theory advanced by Chinese scholars in the Occident to the effect that Chinese civilization came to a standstill at the beginning of the Christian Era for reasons never fully given, and that subsequent changes were practically negligible. Nothing is more misleading than such a theory as we shall see plainly by taking a casual look at Chinese houses and gardens in retrospect.

The terms houses and gardens will be given a somewhat special connotation in this brief note. We shall not attempt a connected story of Chinese architecture in general, for that is a voluminous subject and should be treated only by competent specialists. Nor shall we pause especially to describe imperial palaces, parks and gardens, because they are not representative of Chinese homes. The Emperors themselves were in the habit of considering their homes as being co-extensive with the empire, their luxurious palace units therefore being only selected nooks in the "home." Similarly, public buildings like monasteries, temples, etc., will not be discussed except in so far as they have influenced the planning of the commoner's house and the laying out of his garden.

And the commoner is a very elusive individual in Chinese society. As China's hereditary aristocracy broke up and ceased to exist as a permanent class before the Christian Era, social stratification has been an endless flux. "Great wealth seldom abides in the same house for three generations," so goes the common saying; and the same might be said of official prominence and political influence. Everybody therefore was a commoner and could rise above the general average for a time. The representative commoner was one who typified this flux—a life which combined in its various stages, the lives of the scholar, the official, the farmer, fisher, or wood-cutter.

3

CHINESE HOUSES AND GARDENS

The ancient Chinese people, who built up their civilization in the North temperate zone, where the struggle against the forces of nature was protracted and severe, were simple, hard-working, and practical folk. Their houses and gardens, like all other cultural accomplishments of theirs, bore the impress of their life and mind. The typical farmer's home, after society had become definitely patriarchal, probably consisted of a humble cottage of several rooms, built of wood, shells, or sun-dried bricks, with a thatched or tiled roof; a barn; a garden mainly vegetable; and oftentimes a thrashing yard. Windows were not unknown, though crude, pottery jars with their bottoms broken off often being used as frames. Doors were equally simple, pieces of rope often taking the place of hinges. Wells were sometimes found near private houses, but were usually owned by the communities. Mulberry trees were planted near the house, not as much for beauty and shade as for sericulture, which was the occupation of the women. In a word, the ancient Chinese house was a picture of severe rustic simplicity and the purpose which it was made to serve was purely utilitarian. When and where nature was not particularly kind and lavish in its gifts to men, subsistence necessarily preceded esthetic enjoyment.

Meanwhile, a change gradually took place in China which was to produce far-reaching effects on the physical, as well as the mental aspects of the Chinese home. This is the consolidation of the Chinese classical family system, which became the basic unit of social and political organization, which cultivated a special set of "family" virtues, filial piety included, and which made the Chinese people home-lovers *par excellence*.

The impress of this system upon the material aspects of the Chinese homes was no less apparent. Bigger houses, which were multiplications of the small unit on one site, were demanded to accommodate the bigger family-communities. Units and structures within the house became less immediately utilitarian. On the whole, however, the commoner's homestead remained simple even during the Age of the Poets (8th to 6th century B. C.). Most farmers were still too busy during the working months to bestow much attention on their houses as they usually had to stay in small huts near their fields. Hence the poet sang:

> *The locust in the fifth month bats its thighs;*
> *And in the sixth, its wings the spinner plies.*
> *The next, we find the crickets in the field;*
> *Under our eaves, the eighth, they lie concealed;*
> *The ninth, they come and near our doorways keep;*
> *The tenth, beneath our beds they slyly creep.*
> *The rats we smoke out; chinks we fill up tight;—*
> *And close each opening on the north for light,*
> *And plaster wicker doors; then each one says,*
> *"O wife and children, this year's toiling days*
> *Are o'er, and soon another year will come;*
> *Enter and dwell in this our cozy home."*

Of these little huts, the farmers were no less proud:

The central plot the huts contains,
While gourds each path and boundary line.
Their fruits preserved, aside we put,
Till 'mong the offerings they shall shine.

When the farmer was forced into military service for his lord, his love of home waxed even greater:

To the hills of the east we went,
And long had we there to remain.
When the word of recall was sent,
Thick and fast came the drizzling rain.
On ant hills screamed cranes with delight;
In their rooms were our wives sighing sore.
Our homes they had swept and made tight;—
All at once we arrived at the door.
And bitter gourds hanging are seen,
From branches of chestnut trees high.
Three years of toil away we had been,
Since such a sight greeted the eye.

When Confucius was living, China's material civilization was sufficiently advanced so that most people looked for greater comfort in their private abodes, as well as for more delicacies in their meals. Thus, Confucius praised his disciple Yen Hui who was apparently an exception. "Admirable indeed was the virtue of Hui!" said the Master. "With a single bamboo dish of rice, a single gourd dish of drink, and living in his mean narrow lane, while others could not have endured the distress, he did not allow his joy to be affected by it. Admirable indeed was the virtue of Hui!" Although commentators on the Confucian *Analects* have differed on the interpretation of another passage in the text, it seems believable, according to one school of interpretation, that Tsai Yu, another disciple of Confucius, was once interested in frescoing the walls of his bed-room. Whereupon the Master said, "Rotten wood cannot be carved; a wall of dirty earth will not receive the trowel. This Yu! —what is the use of my reproving him?" It is not unreasonable to suppose that even Confucius' own disciples were interested in physical comfort, at least to a certain degree.

Although we are not interested here primarily in princes and emperors, we should at least recall the single instance of the park of King Wen of the Chou Dynasty who, according to traditional chronology, flourished in the 12th Century B. C., and who was praised by later poets for having shared the enjoyment of his park and buildings with his subjects. Thus the poets sang:

5

When Wen to build his wondrous tower began,
Of all its scheme a plan he drew.
To do the work, in crowds the people ran,
And as by magic, lo! it grew.
"Be not in haste,"—so kindly said the king,
But all as to a father help would bring.

The king was walking in his wondrous park,
Where lay the does, all sleek and clean.
'Twas sweet to him their restfulness to mark,
And see the white birds' glistening sheen.
Then to his wondrous pond he took his way
To view the fish their bounding life display.

Right in the middle of a circling pool,
His hall, the place of joy, he reared.
For music there he made provision full.
'Twixt pillars finely carved appeared
Face boards, with tops of finest tracery,
'Neath which large drums and bells were hang-
ing free.

On these the blind musicians did their part.
Of lizard skin the drums are made.
The eyeless men displayed consummate art;
In perfect unison they played.
The music loud resounded through the hall.
What rapture did the festive throng enthrall! *

In spite of the fact that these stanzas were often recited for the benefit and emulation of feudal potentates, the latter were seldom willing like King Wen to share their joys with their subject commoners. It is little wonder that for a long time the palaces and parks of the sovereigns exercised very little influence upon the humble houses and gardens of the commoners. Moreover, the social usages of feudalism, which insisted on clear demarcations of ranks, set specific and detailed regulations concerning articles of clothing and housing. Unwarranted imitation of one's superior was therefore a violation of the principle of social equilibrium. Even the able feudal minister Kuan Chung, whom Confucius had praised for his success in saving the Middle Kingdom from barbarizations, could not escape the censure of the Chinese Sage in this respect:

The Master said, "Small indeed was the capacity of Kuan Chung," . . . "Then, did Kuan Chung know the rules of propriety?" The Master said, "The princes of States have a screen intercepting the view at their gates. Kuan had likewise a screen at his gate. The princes of States on any friendly meeting between two of them, had a stand on which to place their inverted cups. Kuan had also such a stand. If Kuan knew the rules of propriety, who does not know them?"

---

* Quotations from the *Book of Poetry* and the *Analects* made in these pages are Legge's Translation.

Chinese Houses and Gardens in Retrospect

If regulations in feudal society were strict on screens and stands, how much stricter were they certainly on the construction of houses and on laying out gardens?

Despite rigid feudal regulations, the ancient Chinese found satisfaction in their home-steads and succeeded in affecting harmony between Man and Nature in their houses and gardens. The house is for man and the garden is for nature. It is true that the gardens mentioned by the early poets and philosophers were mainly vegetable gardens; but even a certain amount of utilitarianism could not bar nature out. As early as the sixth century B. C., Laotzu had taught men to return to nature. And Confucius, in spite of his practical mind, said: "The wise find pleasure in water; the virtuous find pleasure in hills." From the time of Laotzu and Confucius, the Chinese people had become nature-conscious—not only philosophically, but also esthetically.

It was not until after the unification of the empire and the introduction of Buddhism however, that Chinese houses and gardens underwent the most important changes. The real unification of the empire in the third century B. C. and particularly the consolidation of the empire in 206 gave rise to possibilities for the greater production and distribution of wealth. The disappearance of the feudal aristocracy was a comparative social liberation. And Buddhism, which had certainly infiltrated into China prior to A. D. 65 —a date set for its official introduction into China—was to exercise extensive and profound influences on Chinese houses and gardens.

The two milleniums that separate us from the great social and political event known as the unification of the empire have wrought numerous important changes in Chinese houses and gardens. Instead of following the development of these two aspects of the Chinese home through its various stages, which would be tedious and hardly feasible on account of the lack of learned treatises on the subject, let us propose to forego a strictly chronological treatment. It seems more pertinent that we summarize the chief influences at work in China's cultural developments and suggest how these forces have acted on houses and gardens in particular.

The first factor with which we have to reckon is the political unification of the empire itself. Before the third century B. C., the unity of the Chinese Empire existed only in the dreams of political thinkers and ambitious feudal lords. After the actual unification, huge architectural plans were projected and executed by the imperial houses. The palatial establishments of the Ch'in Dynasty were so elaborate and extensive that with the fall of the dynasty and the arrival of the rebellious forces, it took the flames of an arson fully three months to reduce them to ashes. The hall of the anterior unit, famous to posterity as O-fang Palace, was said to have been spacious enough to seat ten thousand people. Although few later dynasties could vie with the Ch'in Dynasty in architectural magnificence, each major dynasty had its own period of activities in the construction of palaces and the beautification of the imperial capital.

Partly in line with plans to build up a magnificent capital and concentrate wealth and partly to forestall movements of political dissension and revolt, the early emperors of each new dynasty invariably ordered the removal of the leading families from the provinces to the capital. Aside from political and economic results, this concentration of the most wealthy families gave rise to attractive mansions and pleasure gardens in the chief city of the empire. The capital became not only the centre of politics but also of art and fashion. Hence the greatest gardens of the empire, as a rule, clustered around the capital and became standards for the admiration and imitation of the provincials. The rise and fall of dynasties in China, therefore, explained the flourishing and the desolation of houses and gardens in general.

The transference of the imperial capital, moreover, was usually accompanied by the migration of the centre of beautiful houses and gardens. During the T'ang Dynasty (A. D. 618-906), for example, the best garden-houses were found in Ch'angan (the present day Sian). During the political disorder and the ravaging warfare of the Five Dynasties (907-959) all these fine gardens were reduced to ruins or left to desolation. After the founding of the Sung Dynasty in 960 with its new capital in K'aifeng, the centre of the new garden-houses moved southeastward. And when North China was lost to the Khitans in 1225 and the Sung Imperial Court was moved to south of the Yangtze, the culture of the empire in its entirety, including amusements and customs as well as the art of building garden-houses, was transferred to Hangchow, its new capital. During the period of the Mongol domination (1279-1368), Hangchow, it is true, was no longer the imperial capital, but it remained the leading city of culture and decidedly more refined and more Chinese than Khanbalic (Peip'ing, Peking), which was the seat of the Khan's government. Meanwhile, the East China seaboard had become the wealthiest portion of the empire and remained the home of the most exquisite garden-houses.

In the second place, Buddhism's influence and its transformation of the Chinese outlook on life and nature was even more profound. The introduction of this outlandish cult was synchronal not only with the assurance of political unity and the greater diffusion of wealth in China, but also with the gradual acquisition by Chinese culture of a remarkable degree of sophistication. The simple and practical philosophy and modes of life of the ancients rapidly gave way to the invading culture. A greater appreciation of the beauties of nature was stimulated by the monasteries and pagodas which began to adorn the hill sides. Leisurely pilgrimages were undertaken by many people, irrespective of social station. New architectural conceptions and new symbols in decorative art were gradually adopted.

The best known literary testimony to this profound influence of Buddhism on the Chinese garden-house is probably Yang Hsuan-Chih's *Description of the sangha-arama of Lo-Yang* (Loyang Chialan Chi), a book telling of the leading monasteries in and near the famous city. Loyang was the capital of the Northern Tobar Dynasty, and the Tobars had been converted *en masse* to the Hindu faith. After the fall of the dynasty, many of the monasteries were dilapidated. Yang, who flourished during the second half of the sixth dynasty, was so greatly touched by these beautiful edifices and their surrounding scenery that he wrote a most vivid description of them, which has become a masterpiece of descriptive literature. Writings like Yang's could not but deepen the already prevalent appreciation of natural beauty as taught by the ancients. The influence of Buddhism on the Chinese landscape, however, was not only exerted through the printed page.

The indebtedness of Chinese painting to Buddhism is well known and need not be discussed here. It is interesting to note, however, that art and reality for a long time reacted upon each other. The site for a monastery or a pagoda was selected with the greatest care. Prominence was not the only consideration. The edifice was usually erected where it would best fit into the surrounding landscape so as to form the most harmonious and artistic picture. The architects tried hard to see with the eyes of the painters. And painters, in their turn, were inspired by the visions of the architects. Lovers of garden-houses naturally learned from both architects and painters in their own plans and executions.

Although originally Buddhist in inspiration, this love of natural scenery and beautiful landscapes was so universal that it ceased to be identified with the Buddhist religion alone. Taoism, which plagiarized the Hindu Cult in more than one way, followed suit by building its temples close to nature. And every Chinese, including the professed followers of Confucius, was a Taoist after a fashion. It is not surprising, then, that in all Chinese garden-houses, an effort was made to harmonize Nature with Man and to achieve, only on a reduced scale or in a modified form, that harmonious beauty which characterized the sites of temples and monasteries.

Of course not every Chinese home could boast of a house and a garden. Those who could afford it, would naturally be glad to follow the advice of Hsueh Yeh-ho, who said it was desirable for a private house to consist of three parts of water (lagoons, streamlets, ponds, etc.), two parts devoted to bamboo groves, and one part for the house. Or, they might even go further and follow the advice of Cheng Yu-Wen, author of *Ch'ing Hsien Kung;* and their homes might contain winding footpaths, level terraces lined with fresh flowers, tall pines, quaint rocks, simple pavilions, perilous-looking bridges, slender ditches, deep hills, and gurgling streams besides the regular houses. Those who were less fortunate, however, could always own yards; and substitutes for elaborate gardens were available in miniature gardens. A miniature landscape garden of this nature usually occupied only a few square feet, and the owner could rely on his esthetic imagination and reduce himself to Liliputian stature and take his daily stroll around the garden imaginatively to admire every detail of beauty—pavilions, monasteries, bridges, trees, streams, and what-not that could be found in the natural-sized landscape garden! And this was a boon to the scholar, who was as a rule not too rich to realize his esthetic dreams.

The discussion of the poor scholar leads us conveniently to a consideration of the third potent factor in determinating the basic traits of the representative Chinese home, namely, the rise of the scholar class in China. Just as the farmer was the typical commoner in ancient China, so the scholar represented the cross-section of Chinese society in later times. The scholars were a definite class, but not a caste; as farmers, woodcutters, as well as officials and merchants could also at will become scholars. They represented a tradition, a school of taste, and a station in the endless social flux, and as such, were influential. Their insistence of a simple life was unmistakably reflected in Chinese homes, and the note of simplicity was a healthy and effective check to the increasing elaborateness and artificiality of Chinese houses and gardens.

Simplicity of the home was adhered to as an esthetic and moral ideal. Thus, Wu Yin-Chih of the Tsin Dynasty was noted for his humble abode of a few *mou* of land, with six simple thatched cottages, mean walls and fences. When the great general Liu Pu proposed to build him a new house as a gift, he persistently declined the offer. Likewise, Chang Chih-ho, a poet-painter of the eighth century who styled himself "Fisherman on Bemisted Waves," felt perfectly contented in his home on the eastern suburb of Shao Hsing, a humble house with rough hewn beams and pillars, thatched with green grass. When Yen Chench'ing, noted calligraphist, statesman and general, approached him about the gift of a new house, Chang preferred to remain where he was.

Even when poor scholars had arisen to high official distinction, many of them would still consider it their duty to remain faithful to their ideal of simple living and a simple home.

The three distinguished ministers of the Sung Dynasty, for example, were all known for their indifference to houses and gardens. When Fan Chung-Yen (989-1052) was on the eve of his retirement from public life, his sons and nephews all urged him to repair his house and garden in Loyang so that the aged statesman might spend his last years in comfort. In reply, Fan compared human life to a temporary sojourn and expressed satisfaction with the simplicity of his house as it was. Again, Wang Anshih (1012-80), equally famous as scholar, statesman, and poet, on his resignation from the second term of his premiership, chose to live in a humble cottage near the suburb of Nanking. The cottage was described by contemporaries as "isolated from other houses, barely strong enough to withstand the forces of storms and winds, unprotected with an enclosing wall, and looking very much like a way-side inn." Wang's political opponent Ssuma Kuang (1019-86), great statesman and historian, owned a more picturesque home but his life was equally simple. The Ssuma home boasted of an islet planted with willows, a storeyed building housing the books given the family by three successive emperors, an "Await-Moon Pavilion" near the lagoon, and a few cottages scattered about in the compound. But the premier had only one old servant, who went to bed on the second stroke of the first watch (about 7:30 p.m.) while he himself would read and write until midnight.

The simplicity of house and garden did not fail to satisfy many scholars, because to the philosophically minded, the whole world was a garden and the beauties of nature— fleeting clouds, picturesque sunsets, clear moonlight and refreshing breezes—were every- body's property. One did not have to own a garden in order to enjoy it. It was, therefore, probably not by pure coincidence that Shao Yung (1011-77), the Taoist-Confucian mystic, chose to build his humble cottage in Loyang opposite a garden not his own. Obviously for a similar reason, Wang Hsi-Chih (321-379) the great calligraphist, like numerous others through the ages, built his cottage on a mountain.

The great poet Su Tungp'o (1036-1101) went even further. Upon his return from exile on Hainan Island, he decided to live in Yanghsien, a district famous for its beautiful scenery. For a long time, he succeeded in making only one friend, Shao Minchan, who had come to him as a pupil. And the story continues as follows:

> *Shao succeeded in spotting a house for Su Tungp'o which the latter bought at the price of five hundred strings of cash, an amount which the poet could barely afford after emptying all his bags. A date was finally selected for moving into that house. One evening as he was taking a walk in moonlight with Shao to a village, they heard the voice of a woman sobbing. Tungp'o stopped to listen to it and said, "Why, her voice betrays extreme sorrow! Isn't it likely that she is experiencing the loss of something dear to her? Let me ask her and find out."*
>
> *Accompanied by Shao, he pushed open the gate; and on entering the house, he saw an old woman who continued weeping despite the appearance of the strangers. Tungp'o asked why she was so sorrowful, and she said: "I owned a house which had been handed down from one generation to another for a hundred years. Now my son, the black sheep, has sold it. I moved here today, leaving my century-old homestead forever, and that is why I wept." On hearing this, the poet was deeply moved. He asked where her former home was and discovered that it was the very house which he had just bought for five hundred strings of cash. Whereupon he immediately consoled her by saying, "It is I who have bought your home. But don't feel sad; I am going to return it to you." He sent for the deed and burned it in her presence. He summoned the son and asked him to bring his mother back to the old house, and to forget about the strings of cash. After that, the poet returned to Piling and never bought another house.*

It goes without saying that this ideal of simple living and a simple home was not followed persistently. Rich people, especially social upstarts, have always found it diffi- cult to conform. Shih Ch'ung (249-300), for example, not only built the most luxurious mansions of the time, but also vied with the aristocrat Wang K'ai in the acquisition of the most precious furnishings. When Wang K'ai had ordered the erection of a shaded walk forty *li* in length covered with colored silk, Shih Ch'ung built a similar walk fifty *li* long and used brocade in place of ordinary silk.. It is no wonder that when the latter paid a visit to the sacrificial hall of the Confucian Temple, he entertained but little respect for Confucius' greatest disciple, Yen Huei, who had been contented with windows framed by broken jars.

In the seventh century, especially after the Empress Dowager Wu (684-705) rose to power by usurpation, beautiful mansions with elaborate gardens grew up like mushrooms in the metropolitan district of Ch'angan. When the wealthy opportunist Wang Hung was ordered by imperial decree to take his own life, he had acquired so much real property that officials in charge of its confiscation had to spend several days in making a mere inventory of his houses and gardens. His own home was the last word in luxury and extravagance. An interesting structure was his "Automatic-Rain pavilion" which kept the air cool even during the intense heat of summer.

To people like these the ideal of the simple life apparently made no appeal and the esthetic censure meted out by scholars which branded them as "vulgar" was no effective threat. More practical checks, however, were found in popular superstitions. Of these, let us mention two: geomancy and ghost-lore.

Geomancy, in brief, was a set of superstitious principles governing the location, the direction, the plan of arrangement, and even the size of an architectural edifice—applicable to a tomb as well as to a house. The violation of these principles, it was believed, would bring catastrophe to individuals and families. Thus, even at the time of Confucius, a belief had grown up that extensions of houses toward certain directions would bring bad luck to the owners and occupants. From that time on, geomancy became more occult and grew in potency and complexity, so that the greatest care was usually exercised even in placing a weather-cock on top of one's house.

The power of ghost-lore in this respect is self-explanatory. Evil spirits, besides inflicting punishments on those whose houses and gardens had been acquired in a dishonorable way, would reside in those establishments to make the enjoyment of them impossible. Although it would be interesting to retell some of the ghost stories relating to houses and gardens, it behooves us to confine our interest to Man and Nature alone.

Chinese houses and gardens were on the whole an indigenous development in China, even Buddhism having had to undergo a process of sinanization before its influence was widely felt. But like the main body of Chinese culture itself, however, houses and gardens in China have always admitted foreign influences. During all the major periods of economic prosperity and political security in Chinese history, the Chinese were usually active and enthusiastic in making cultural borrowings and assimilations. To return to the realm of our immediate interest, we should note that the earliest period of Buddhist architecture and landscape gardening in China was essentially foreign in inspiration and design. In later times, the repeated reassertion of the Chinese genius in the appropriation of cultural loans from neighboring regions succeeded as a rule in effacing all discordant exoticisms. The pagoda, for example, has been so modified and become so peculiarly Chinese that its resemblance to its Hindu prototype could only be detected by expert eyes.

The pagoda, however, is not an isolated instance. Units of the arabesque architecture were introduced during the eighth century and some specimens are still visible in the city of Canton today. With the pagoda also came various art-motifs from India, among which the swastika and the wheel of transmigration were particularly noteworthy. Based on these as patterns, indigenous *motifs* were evolved: for example, the conventionalized forms of the character for longevity; the bat, in Chinese homonymous with the word for blessing; the ornamental representations of the characters for good luck 吉 and happiness 喜; and the fairy peach, symbol of longevity.

Many articles of furniture in the house were doubtless adaptations from "lands in the West"—for the most part regions now known as Tibet and Turkestan. In the second century of our era, Emperor Ling of the Han Dynasty was noted for his enthusiasm for "foreign furniture," especially for foreign chairs, foreign canopies and foreign couches, and these couches have been known in China to this day by their original name of *Hu Ch'uang*. By the sixth century, when the use of furniture became universal, the foreign origin of many types of furniture had already been lost! Another foreign commodity which transformed the Chinese house was glass. Crystals were known in China in antiquity, and glasswares were not uncommon among members of the royal house and the aristocrats during the first centuries of the Christian Era. According to the late Dr. Berthold Laufer of the Field Museum, however, glass plates were not used in China in large quantities until the fifth century. The revolutionary changes in the construction of doors, windows, grills, dormers, and screens, and in the accompanying lattice work need no elaboration. Moreover, the use of glass plates, though never displacing the use of paper in this respect, made it readily possible in winter to appreciate the beauty of the garden from within the house; and house and garden were more closely knitted into a single unit of the home than ever before.

The garden, likewise, was to benefit from foreign importations. The following are especially interesting: grapes, or *Putao* in Chinese, which betrays its Greek origin (Botrus); pomegranates; the walnut, known as *Hutao* in Chinese, literally the "foreign peach"; the jasmine; the peony, which soon after its introduction became the "king" of all flowers. All through the Middle Ages, exchange of flowers and fruits, plants and vegetables between China and the Iranian world was particularly noticeable and has been ably and fully treated by Dr. Laufer in his book entitled *Sino-Iranica*.

Another wave of foreign influence on Chinese houses and gardens was exerted through the Jesuits in China during the seventeenth and eighteenth centuries. The greatest monument to this Occidental influence was the "Far Western Unit" in the old Summer

Palace Yuanming Yuan which was destroyed after a thorough looting by British and French troops only less than a century ago. This Occidental unit was built during the reign of Ch'ien Lung (1736-96) under the supervision of Jesuit missionaries in the Chinese Court, especially Attiret, Benoist, and Castiglione. As summarized by Dr. Carroll Brown Malone,*

> The rococo architecture of these palace buildings recalls the extravagance of Italian art at the end of the 17th century as seen in the work of Borromini, Guarini, and Bibiena. . . . Ch'ien Lung's European palaces contained numerous false windows and doors, excessive ornamentation in carved stone, glazed tiles in startling color combinations, imitation shells and rock-work, meaningless pyramids, scrolls and foliage, and conspicuous outside staircases, not uncommon in the buildings of contemporary Europe. The parts of the gardens nearest to the buildings were laid out in a very formal manner, with conventionally trimmed trees and symmetrically paved paths. But, in spite of obvious architectural faults, these buildings contained many a splendid view and many an exquisite detail. The formality of the various scenes was relieved by some good Chinese rockeries and by the natural beauty of the large trees on the nearby hills.

Western architecture in Yuanming Yuan is of interest to us not only because it was a curious piece of decoration in the Imperial Summer Palace, but also because it was a source of information and a living example to those who cared to build in the Western style. Foreign houses and gardens in Canton had been built in imitation of the "factories" and co-hongs and probably owed little to Yuanming Yuan. With the frequent visits of Emperor Ch'ien Lung to East China, especially to the vicinity of Yangchow, this new interest in Western architecture spread to the Yangtze region.

A building near the Green-Willow Bay in Yangchow, for example, was a reflection of this imitative taste.

> In front was a verandah, fenced with a balustrade. Behind that was a spacious hall which appeared like a thousand suites of rooms. Each turn around the house gave one a new sense of bewilderment. One would hear the chime of bells and make his turns accordingly; because there was a clock in the building and the bells would synchronize with each turn one took. On one wall were paintings of mountains and rivers, oceans and islands. On the opposite there was a mirror under a light, which reflected the painted scenes. Above was a dormer, which allowed sky-light and cloud-shadows, sunshine or moonlight to add their parts to the exquisite sight.

Besides a beautiful fountain at the Water-and-Bamboo cottage of Hsu Li-An, houses and gardens in East China also boasted of Western walls, Western pedestals, Western buttresses, and Western screens.

We must note, in this connection, that Western architecture in China was not a one-sided influence. Europe also played its part to complete the circuit of cultural reci-

---

* *History of the Peking Summer Palaces under the Ch'ing Dynasty*, Urbana, Illinois, 1934, p. 160.

procity by building houses and laying out gardens "after the Chinese fashion." With the importation of the numerous *chinoiseries* into Europe, and with the natural decline of the Dutch school of gardening, a new taste grew up in the Occident generally referred to as the Anglo-Chinese style of garden planning which began in England under the leadership of Sir William Chambers, and later spread to Continental Europe. I have written on this phase of our subject elsewhere and shall not rehearse the details.* Let it suffice, therefore, to reproduce here a piece of contemporary testimony which I have not quoted before. The following lines are from a poem written by James Cawthorn in 1756 entitled "Of Taste: An Essay Spoken at the Anniversary Visitation of Tunbridge School, 1756":

> *Of late, 'tis true, quite sick of Rome and Greece,*
> *We fetch our models from the wise Chinese:*
> *European artists are too cold and chaste,*
> *For Mand'rin only is the man of taste;*
> *Whose golden genius, fondly wild to see*
> *His grove a forest, and his pond a sea,*
> *Breaks out . . . . . and, whimsically great, designs*
> *Without the shackles of rules or lines.*
> *Form'd on his plans, our farms and seats begin*
> *To match the boasted villas of Pekin.*
> *On ev'ry hill a spire-crown'd temple swells,*
> *Hung around with serpents, and a fringe of bells:*
> *Junks and balons along our waters sail,*
> *With each a gilded cock-boat at his tail;*
> *Our choice exotics to the breeze exhale*
> *Within th' enclosure of a zig-zag rail;*
> *In Tartar huts our cows and horses lie*
> *Our hogs are fatter in an Indian stye;*
> *On ev'ry shelf a Joss divinely stares,*
> *Nymphs laid on chintzes sprawl upon our chairs;*
> *While o'er our cabinets Confucius nods,*
> *'Midst porcelain elephants and china gods.*

It is curious that this experiment in cultural interchange between Europe and China did not prove very successful to either party.

After outlining these several factors which have transformed and reshaped houses and gardens in China through the ages, from the simple homesteads of the ancient farmers to artistic garden houses such as are presented in this album, it seems pertinent that we ask one more question. With the onslaught of Occidental culture in China, resulting in the prevalence of Western architecture in all the principal cities of the East, what will be

---

* See "The Chinese Garden in Eighteenth Century England" in the *T'ien Hsia Monthly*, April 1936.

the future of Chinese houses and gardens? In one of his observations made of contemporary China, Mr. E. R. Hughes of the University of Oxford has implied an answer:*

> In the field of architecture the same electic spirit can now be seen coming into play. In the first instance the growth of cities like Shanghai and the other ports involved the use of Western architecture for factories, offices, banks, hotels, and so on. Buildings such as these originally built by foreigners, have been copied by Chinese firms, until today the main streets in any port differ very little at first sight from those in any foreign town, except for the Chinese signs which still hang in the old way outside the modern shops. There is, however a tendency on the part of the Chinese builder to take the old patterns and express them in plaster ornamentations. These may appear somewhat rococo to the Western eye, but there is in them something of the old Chinese artistry trying to express itself in the new medium. Experiments in combining the colorful Chinese roofs and eaves with modern-style two- and three- storey buildings of reinforced concrete have been made . . .

What has been said of public buildings and commercial establishments is also generally true, on a lesser scale, of Chinese houses and gardens.

Architecturally as well as in a thousand other ways, then, Young China seems to believe in the eventual and inevitable realization of a world culture, to which she must contribute and in which she must lose herself temporarily. For her part, she has become an enthusiastic and willing pupil of the West, confident of her ability to retain the best of the old while absorbing the new. Whether China has anything worthy of her cultural heritage to contribute to the West in the way of houses and gardens, it remains for the Occident to decide for itself.

---

* *The Invasion of China by the Western World,* London and New York, 1938, p. 273.

Foreign Influence in
Chinese Architecture

By Chuin Tung, M. Arch.

TO the Hellenic World China was known as early as the fourth century B.C., but simply as the land celebrated for sericulture. The Chinese people, on the other hand, did not even bother to inquire who consumed their silk, which later in imperial Rome was worth its weight in gold.

Gibbon, in *The Decline and Fall of the Roman Empire*, deplored that the art of printing failed to reach Europe with the importation of silk. However, long before Europe received the blessing of printing, Greek influence had already firmly established itself, though indirectly, in Chinese art.

Official communication between the Roman and Chinese Empires, according to Chinese records, took place in A.D. 166, but neither one seemed to have made any impression whatsoever on the other through the contact. This does not mean that China was entirely free from foreign influence at that time, for a century earlier the Han Emperor Mingti (A.D. 58-75), inspired by Buddhism, had dispatched delegates to India, and immediately afterwards Hindu monks came to the capital, Loyang. Here the first Buddhist temple, Pai Ma Sze (White Horse Temple), was built. The importance of this temple lies more in nomenclature than style. The building, though a Buddhist shrine, was not a reproduction of Hindu architecture. Meanwhile, the word "Sze," which had hitherto meant a governmental department, was now employed also to designate a Buddhist temple. This usage became gradually an accepted one, with the result that today it is the exclusive term for all the monastic Buddhist temples in China.

The development of a certain coloured material, peculiar to Chinese architecture, also began in the Han Dynasty. This glittering and translucent material, *liu li*—a term derived from the Sanskrit "vaidurya"—created a new craze and was much treasured by the Chinese in the second century B. C. It was imported through the southwest into China, and first mentioned in *Hsi Ching Tsa Chi* (Miscellaneous Records of the Western Capital) as building material, in the form of a glazed screen, which, more concealing than transparent, much delighted an imperial concubine. This material was developed five hundred years later into the glazed tile which became indispensable in roofing the palace buildings in imperial style.

The stone tablets in Wu Liang T'zu, a family shrine, executed in the second century

A.D., give some valuable information in bas-relief regarding Chinese architecture in the Han Dynasty. An instance is the playful figure on the second storey of a building, balancing on his hands a portion of the roof. Strangely enough the supporting is also done by the head, very similar to the Caryatid in Greek architecture. The difference is that while the Chinese acrobat seems to be in a jovial mood, the Caryatid is supposed to be fulfilling the duty of a slave, in shame, sorrow, and servitude. It might be far-fetched to suggest that the Chinese relief was inspired by the Hellenic legend, but the resemblance is indeed striking.

The guardian of the Chinese temple gate, the stone lion, made its appearance in the Han Dynasty. A most remarkable example now stands in front of the tomb of Kao Yi, in Szechuan, executed about A.D. 209. Our particular interest is not so much concerned with whether the animal is a lion, as with the strong similarity it bears to the Assyrian winged bull. The fact that the latter was also used to flank the Assyrian palace portal makes the resemblance all the more extraordinary.

The year A.D. 366 witnessed the beginning of the rock-cut Cave of a Thousand Buddhas at Tunhuang, and marked the commencement in China of a period of more than two centuries of active cave-cutting, which thoroughly displayed the intensity of religious fervour. Other well-known caves followed, at Yun Kang, A.D. 409; Lung Men, A.D. 494; and T'ien Lung Shan, A.D. 575. Lesser caves are numerous, and the rock-cutting activity did not entirely cease till the end of the Yuan Dynasty (A.D. 1279-1368). In these caves one discovers the development of sculpture from the Greco-Indian-Gandhara tradition to the pure T'ang Dynasty style. At Yun Kang is to be found the polygonal column with an Ionic capital. There are also such architectural ornaments as the acanthus, honey suckle, garland, and "egg and dart." All these evidences point to the wholesale influx of Hellenistic influence through India. The Indian characteristic is the strongest at T'ien Lung Shan. Quite likely Hindu craftsmen played an important part in its construction.

During the "Six Dynasties" (A.D. 220-589) a conspicuous tomb ornament is the stone pillar, standing side by side with the stone lion. In many cases the main part of the shaft is fluted, in exactly the same style as the Greek Doric column. The fact that this type of ornament exists mainly to the south of the Yangtze might prove the growing popularity of another channel through which Western influence came to China—the sea route.

Although the picture of a pagoda, known in India as the *stupa,* was said to be painted on the fresco at Pai Ma Sze in the Han Dynasty, it is doubtful whether a pagoda was actually built at this time. Pagoda construction was recorded in the middle of the third century A.D., but existing ancient examples have yet to be found in the various rock-cut caves. One of the earliest pagodas, and the grandest, is described in *Loyang Chialan Chi.* This pagoda of Yung Ning Sze, built in A.D. 516, was nine storeys high and of wooden construction. The fact that a structure was built to the somewhat exaggerated height of 900 feet* and was accomplished with timber, is most significant. The Hindu *stupa,* invariably erected with masonry, was now transformed by the Chinese architectural genius into an entirely different system of construction. The Chinese pagoda thus became as organic as, and akin to, the Chinese palace and temple.

We see all kinds of Chinese pagodas today, and it is difficult to classify them. Well known is the Great-Goose Pagoda in Sian, built of brick about A.D. 625, but with few Chinese features. Sometimes the core of the pagoda is constructed of masonry, sheathed with a wooden facade purely Chinese in character. Most of the pagodas built in masonry have also the Chinese roofing, balcony, and portal, with nothing foreign about them.

In the T'ang Dynasty (618-906) the capital Ch'angan became a melting pot of many nationalities. Arabs, Jews, but mainly Persians, composed the foreign community of the metropolis, and it is important to note that although hitherto India had supplied all the inspiration to Chinese art and religion, new forces from Central Asia now came to affect the mode of living in China. Among other things, the polo game, originated in Persia, became popular in China. "Air-conditioning," an innovation then as now, was installed in the palace of the Emperor Hsuan Tsung (A.D. 712-765). The apparatus, it appears, was designed on the principle of circulation of cold water, and its operation was so successful that, during an audience, although a minister was overcome with shivering, teeth-chattering, and gastric disorder, the sovereign, evidently made of no common clay, thoroughly enjoyed the freezing atmosphere. A few wealthy people in the Capital also availed themselves of this modern convenience, and their homes were constantly enriched with other foreign novelties.

Ch'angan now assumed a cosmopolitan character. Parsees, Manicheans, Mohammedans and Nestorians rubbed shoulders with one another, and worshipped in their respective temples. As foreign craftsmen undoubtedly played their part in the construction of these buildings, new foreign architectural elements were inevitably introduced. A Persian monk, Chien Chen, even journeyed from China to Japan to build a temple there—the now well-known T'ang Chao Ti Sze (Toshodaiji, A.D. 759). This monument is important as it is typical of T'ang Dynasty architecture. A salient feature is the entasis of the column, one of the many Greek architectural refinements which the Persians were possibly instrumental in bringing to the Far East.

The carved stone base seen in monumental Chinese architecture, technically called Hsu Mi Tso, owes its origin to a Greco-Indian motif, which resembles the classical pedestal with its dado stunted. It first appeared in the rock-cut caves, but was not adopted as the base of a building until the "Six Dynasties." The Sung Dynasty (A.D. 960-1278) stand-

---

* The Chinese foot then was equal to only a little more than half of the English foot.

crowned heads to be inconsistent; for, although the Emperor Ch'ien Lung insisted that the Jesuit painters under his patronage should paint strictly in the Chinese style, in the matter of architecture he desired just the opposite. This stupidity on the part of the Manchu ruler was responsible for a number of garden buildings in the European style, with fountains, parterres, and even a maze—all to be wantonly destroyed later by the French-British forces in 1860. Since this architectural group was on forbidden ground and enjoyed but a brief existence, it was prevented from ever being popularly imitated.

The "foreign building" or *Yang lou*, as Yuan Mei (1716-1797) called it in one of his poems on Canton, ceased to be a curiosity and became a familiar sight after the "treaty ports" had been thrown open to foreigners. Gradually foreign architects came to plan and supervise foreign-owned buildings in these ports, while the Chinese craftsmen served merely as builders and laborers. Large Chinese cities, Shanghai particularly, present a riotous spectacle of architectural styles of all nations and all periods—a phenomenon that greatly confuses the observer today.

From India and the West, China has received much architecturally but given little. Even the great Buddhist Hsuan Chuang (circa 605-665), who travelled in India for sixteen years, made not a single contribution to Hindu architecture, but was on the contrary quite mindful of bringing back to China, among other things, the design for Great-Goose Pagoda. Architecture in China, with the exception of influencing certain parts of Korean and Japanese buildings, underwent rather a wholesale transplantation. Sir William Chambers was the first European architect charmed by the Chinese building-art, only to be discouraged by Samuel Johnson. Chinese architecture, in spite of Chambers' enthusiasm and the efforts of the French Jesuits, besides freeing the rigid English gardens to some extent, merely succeeded in creating a mild stir in the realm of furniture design, with the appearance of the Chippendale and *Chinoiserie* in eighteenth-century Europe. The superficial observer is invariably captivated by the Chinese architectural ornaments, but blind to the great principle of construction which alone gives them meaning. The Chinese builder never sacrificed the structural for any decoration, however attractive. In all the great epochs of Chinese architecture, the spirit remained distinctly Chinese, no matter how much foreign influence it had assimilated.

Chinese Gardens: Contrasts; Designs

By Chuin Tung, M. Arch.

I. CHINESE AND WESTERN GARDENS CONTRASTED

A French poet once declared, "J'aime fort les jardins qui sentent le sauvage." This just hits upon the difference between Western and Chinese gardens, the latter being entirely devoid of the jungle atmosphere. The Chinese garden is primarily not a single wide open space, but is divided into corridors and courts, in which buildings, and not plant life, dominate. But garden architecture in China is so delightfully informal and playful that even without flowers and trees it would still make a garden. This is especially true of the Japanese garden, which is modelled after the Chinese. In the Ryoan-ji Garden, Kyoto, there is absolutely no plant life, only stone and sand being employed. Its saving grace lies in the thick grove immediately surrounding it. On the other hand, Western gardens consist much more of landscape than of architecture. (Sir William Chambers called them cities of verdure.) The buildings, if any, stand in solitary splendor. Foliage, flowers and fountains are more akin to one another than to the buildings, in spite of the effort to arrange them architecturally, even to the extent of laying them out symmetrically and axially.

The first European who seriously studied Chinese gardens was Sir William Chambers who, in his *Dissertation on Oriental Gardening*, tried to prove the superiority of Chinese gardens. He had the good fortune of coming to China during the reign of the Manchu Emperor Kao Tsung (Ch'ien-lung, 1736-1796), the golden age of the art of Chinese gardening. It is, however, futile to debate upon the relative merits of Chinese and European gardens. So long as each is harmonious with the art, philosophy, and life of its respective world, each is as great as the other.

Standing halfway between the East and West is the Alhambra of Granada. Here one finds a series of courts very similar to those in a Chinese garden, while verdure and water are laid out geometrically and axially in European style. Although symmetry is strongly evident, it has nevertheless none of the rigidity and monotony of Western gardens.

Roman gardens, inspiring the whole of Europe and America, excel especially in terracing and exuberant vegetation provided generously by topography and climate. Parterres, marbles, staircases and cascades are arranged in strong formality. Tall cypresses stand in formidable rows. But with all its axes and repetitions, the Italian garden, by

23

virtue of its successive terraces, does achieve one object—to surprise, which is one of the reasons for which the Chinese garden exists. Entering Villa d'Este at Tivoli, one encounters full corridors and gloomy halls until one suddenly comes upon that superb view which is incomparable. In almost all Chinese gardens the visitor has a similar experience. But instead of a panorama he sees a mere fraction of the whole enchantment, only to be surprised again and again as he wanders on. Terraces in Roman villas, while leading to one elevation after another, have similar spaces, but not different worlds. This element of surprise is completely absent from gardens on a flat ground, such as those in France, for instance, where monotony is heightened by an increase in size.

The Chinese garden is never meant to be monumental. The art of gardening in China is an intimate, human and sophisticated thing, and Chinese gardens seldom have that awe-inspiring but desolate spectacle one usually finds in Western gardens. Even when on a palatial scale a Chinese garden does not lose that intimate quality. On the other hand, Versailles is only saved from looking like a wild desert on crowded Sundays. Symmetry, while observed in monumental and even domestic architecture, is completely disregarded in the lay-out of a Chinese garden, where relaxation, and not reason, rules. This, of course, does not apply to individual buildings themselves in the garden. In all Western gardens, symmetry is indeed carried to such silly extremes that, as Le Notre observed, only the nurse on the second floor could appreciate it from the window. But even Le Notre himself could not entirely break away from its fetters.

The Chinese garden is not built as a playground for a multitude of people. Problems of circulation, which in Western gardens are admirably solved by axes and crossroads, are no problems when men *wander* in the garden, and not *walk through* it. The long corridors, narrow doorways and curved parts in a Chinese garden are not meant for a crowd. The stairs, bridges, and rockery are never designed to please children. It is not a place for recreation. It is essentially for contemplation and solitude.

Although the Chinese garden is a product of sophisticated art, the plant life in it is usually free from any appearance of artifice. Here you find neither trimmed hedges in straight lines, nor flowers arranged in geometric patterns. Whatever fantasies the European landscape architect lavishes upon plants, the Chinese reserves for his garden buildings. Nature is let alone, and yet the Chinese garden never appears *botanical*. Most conspicuous is the absence of the mown and bordered lawn, which, though attractive to the cow, has but little appeal to the human intellect. The planting of majestic cypresses to make an avenue, the clipping of boxwood to shapes like birds and animals, the control of water to jet forth to a certain height, all these seem to be, to borrow a phrase from Wilde, "two touches of Nature." But in spite of these "touches," the Western garden never succeeds in ridding itself of the look of a wilderness.

The aim of the Chinese garden is "to charm, to delight and to give pleasure," and illustrates what may be called the art of deception. I would not go so far as to say that the visitor knows perfectly well he is deceived. The question of reality does not bother him, as soon as he ceases to be in the *garden,* and begins to live in the *picture.* Worlds open out to him; verses and inscriptions carry away his imagination; vistas tempt his curiosity. Every object, in fact, is just as it should appear in a painting. A Chinese garden is indeed a landscape painting in three dimensions, but like Chinese painting, it is subjective.

For one who has seen both Western and Chinese gardens, their effect on the emotions is quite opposite. Who leaves Frascati and Tivoli but must be inspired by the vitality, splendor, and monumentality of those Italian gardens. The Chinese garden does not awe the visitor. It embraces him in its soft charms and intricacies. After the gate is closed behind him, he wakes up from a pleasant dream.

Gardens in Japan, though of Chinese parentage, have more conventions and less complexities in lay-out than the Chinese. The Japanese gardener rarely employs a piece of rock without an eye to its symbolic meaning. He even goes so far as to fashion cascades and pools without using water. Plants are sometimes dwarfed or clipped. But on the whole, the Japanese garden, although it manages to have closed-in vistas, is very much open; and unlike its Chinese prototype, it is not cut up into a maze of courts and corridors. In fact, the Japanese garden resembles the Western in looking like the "forest primeval,"—with this difference, that the Japanese attach to it a mystic significance and have succeeded in it to reduce the Universe into a miniature world.

II. THE DESIGN OF CHINESE GARDENS

The horticulturist has no place in designing a Chinese garden. Neither has the "landscape architect" (a term of purely Western invention), who is concerned with much landscape but little architecture. The poet, the scholar and the monk have in the past shared equal honors in this branch of Chinese art; but above all, to be a good garden-architect one must be a great painter.

Chinese garden-design is primarily a branch of pictorial art. It has neither reason, logic, nor formula. (Not so with the Japanese, who classify gardens into the formal and the informal, which are again divided into the hilly and the flat.) No explanation, for instance, could be offered for paths, verandahs, and bridges planned in zigzag fashion, except that they are picturesque. This oftentimes gives a rococo look to a Chinese garden. But it is also responsible for the exquisite wall tracery and window grills, fantastic doorways and kaleidoscopic pavement patterns. In this respect, the Japanese garden, in its sylvan simplicity, stands in sharp contrast. (Oswald Spengler, in his *The Decline of the West,* identifies the mazy path in Chinese gardens with *tao.* But *tao* in the classics means straightforwardness, or as Confucius said, "acting straight.")

The Chinese garden is usually enclosed in high walls. Its different courts, too, are divided by walls sometimes with porches running along one or both sides. Except where sloping ground does not permit, the wall is vitally necessary for isolating the garden from the rest of the world. In most cases the blank surface of the wall is relieved by a series of traceries, patterned with thin brick or tile, and white-washed. The beauty of the tracery is greatly enhanced by its depth, which, when light plays on it, presents the most sparkling spectacle. The same tracery may look entirely different under light coming from different angles. The variety of tracery design has no limit. In the same garden one seldom finds it repeated.

The garden wall in South China is invariably white-washed. (In the North the garden wall is usually built of rubble stone.) It lends itself admirably to bamboo shadows thrown on it by sunlight or moonlight. White, with green foliage and black roof-tiles and wood-work, forms one of the dominating colors in the Chinese garden. The top of the wall is usually undulated, and relieved of its heaviness by tile-tracery. This idea is sometimes carried too far when head and tail are added to make it look like a dragon.

The wall is seldom straight. Winding and creeping, it may terminate either in a pavilion or a hill. It can stop gracefully in curves or further continue itself with a screen of rockery.

Since the Chinese garden is not a showy art, it depends largely upon the wall to conceal its beauty, beckoning the wanderer on with a glimpse through the doorway or the grille. In the blank wall there also lies a religious significance. (Bodhidharma, the first Zen priest, sat facing a stone wall for nine years.) To the Zen Buddhist it means the end, the ultimate. The entire garden is a retreat for meditation. The Japanese garden, in this respect, has many religious conventions derived from Zen philosophy.

Doorways and window grilles are designed in various ways and are characteristic of the Chinese garden. The doorway is shaped like a moon, a vase or a flower petal. No picture-frame is more attractive than one of these doorways through which a vista arrests the eye. Window grilles, the closeness of whose pattern is necessitated by the rather small size of the translucent sea-shells that serve as panes, assume innumerable forms. The best designs, however, are those strong and simple forms which exclude intricacy.

The pavement in Chinese garden design is made doubly interesting by the employment of insignificant, or even waste, material. Chips of stone, broken tiles, pebbles and fragments of porcelain could make mosaics inexhaustible in pattern and color. Usually the design is symmetrical, in the form of combinations of polygons or quatrefoils. Of the asymetrical forms the most common is the "broken-ice" pattern. It is, however, to border on vulgarity to make such realistic designs as fish, deer, lotus or crane.

Another unique feature is the rockery, on which half of the charm of Chinese gardens usually depends. Nowhere in the whole world is there such a craze for artificial hills.

It is true that in the Western garden one often finds rocks and grottos, and in the Japanese garden, rock-hills and sometimes "suti-ishi" which means random stones. But in all these cases the stone suffers no hydraulic transformation. Even in the Ryoan-ji Garden, Kyoto, where fifteen pieces of rock symbolizing tigers and cubs are to be seen, the stones look no less natural than those in the mountains. Chinese rockery, on the other hand, is in most cases composed of that kind of limestone which derives its fantastic shape through the action of water. Lake rock, as it is usually called (confined to T'ai Hu Lake alone), is quarried from the bottom of lakes where after centuries of washing and scouring it becomes porous, spare, and grotesque. Stones in other regions are also employed. One seldom enters a Chinese garden without seeing rockery, either in the form of peaks, embankments, hills or grottos. Sometimes the rock-hill dominates the entire garden.

Chinese artists are passionately in love with rockery, not only on account of its attractive form, but also because stone in general has that quality of unchangeable solidity which the human character too often lacks. Many celebrated individuals throughout Chinese history are known to be devoted to, or even to worship, rockery. The famous calligraphist and painter Mi Fei of the Sung Dynasty went to the extent of hailing one stone as his "big brother." Another Yuan painter, Ko Chiu-ssu, paid homage to a strange looking rock. This rock now stands in the garden called the "Half-Cocoon" at Quinsan, Kiangsu Province. When stone is endowed with personality, one can find it delightful company.

The first extensive rock garden was built by Emperor Hui Tsung (1101-1125) of the Sung Dynasty, although records date its appearance as early as Han. (Liang Hsiao Wang and Yuan Kuang-han both had gardens in the Han Dynasty.) The Emperor himself being an inimitable painter, lavished his attention much more on rockery than on statecraft. The Emperor built the "Ken Yu," a rock-hill in the Northeast of the capital Kaifeng, between 1117 and 1122. Barges swarmed on the canals, loaded with stones from T'ai Hu Lake. Lake rock was then much treasured, rocks in other localities being much less valued. This tempted people to make lake rock artificially, by laying under turbulent water ordinary rocks carved in the desired shapes, for a certain length of time. The craze for T'ai Hu rocks was at its height during the latter part of the Ming Dynasty. Connoisseurs paid fabulous prices for such pieces reputed to have been authenticated by experts.

During the latter part of the Sung Dynasty, the scholar Yeh Meng-teh of Huchow built an estate almost entirely of rockery, which he poetically called the "Stone Groove." But it was pointed out that a good many of the rocks he found *in situ*, and all he did was to bring them to light by removing the earth around them.

Of all the famous rock-gardens in history, only one has survived. This is the so-called "Lion Garden" in Soochow. The rockery dates back to 1342 A.D., its creator being an abbot.

Rockery, besides being that part of nature which appeals to the cave-man as well as the poet, is indispensable in Chinese garden design. It links admirably plant life and water with the multitude of buildings. Standing halfway between nature and human creation, rockery carries over gracefully the life impulse of the former into the cold artificiality of the latter. The cypresses in an Italian garden, it may be observed, serve a similar purpose, acting as transition from the boxwood to the casino; and they go well with formal architecture, just as rockery does with the informal.

There are several theories about designing the rock-hill. Some strive for magnitude, a mazy stretch of peaks, valleys and grottos. Others concentrate on one small hill only. One man, Chang Nan-yuan during the early Manchu Dynasty, looked down upon the idea of imitating a real hill with a heap of stones. He cared primarily for the casual, the irregular, in nature, and succeeded in emphasizing the essentials or suggesting the existence of a hill, with a minimum amount of rockery. Ko Yu-liang, usually confining his labor to making one hill in a garden and making it well, later improved the construction of grottos. Grottos, it should be noted, had hitherto been customarily made by having the top spanned with slabs of stone. Ko scorned this method, his innovation being a dome top made of converging stones, much resembling a genuine cave.

Both Chi Ch'eng (born 1582) and Li Yu (who called himself Li-Li-weng, lived in the seventeenth century) gave lengthy accounts of the art of rockery. To be a master designer of it one must be a good landscape painter. It is almost impossible to design an extensive rock-hill well. A hill small but exquisite is much more preferable. For this reason the famed "Lion Garden" in Soochow had once the misfortune of being called a "stupendous heap of slag" (See "Six Chapters of a Floating Life," by Shen Fu in the *Tien Hsia Monthly*, Vol. I, August-November, 1935).

One form of playful architecture is to build a pavilion in the manner of a houseboat, standing near the water. Sometimes temporary architectural expedients are devised to meet emergencies, as in the case of a royal prince at the end of the fifth century who had a weakness for gardens. Lest his pleasure ground be observed from his father's palace higher up, he invented folding walls which could screen his earthly paradise at short notice.

There is another instance of a display of ingenuity. Ni Ts'an, a Yuan Dynasty painter, was once invited by his friend to see lotus flowers. Upon his arrival he saw nothing but an empty courtyard. His astonishment, however, was as great as his disappointment when, returning to the same courtyard after the feast, he saw a pond full of lotus. The magic was a simple one. Hundreds of pots of lotus flowers were swiftly placed in the courtyard, which, being slightly sunk, became a pool when a water reservoir discharged just enough water to submerge the pots.

Scholars, when they write about gardens, seldom give adequate accounts of plant life. We may say that plant life is used in the Chinese garden mainly to hide the buildings. Flowers are often mentioned because, besides giving perfume, they are invaluable to poetry, the most aristocratic being peony and *paeonia albiflora*. Lotus, wistaria, plum, laurel, begonia, jasmin and chrysanthemum are common to all gardens. No garden is complete, of course, without the bamboo. The usual evergreens are pine, juniper, and cedar. There is an almost endless variety of trees—willow, maple, *sterculia platanifolia*, palm, musa, elm, and so on. Well known is the ingenuity of the Chinese garden in transplanting and cross-breeding flowers and trees. Plant life in Chinese gardens deserves a separate treatise by the botanist.

Man and Nature in the Chinese Garden

By Wing-Tsit Chan, Ph. D.

THE Chinese garden is more than just flowers and rocks and pavilions; it stands as a monument of triumph of man's effort to find his place in nature and to remain happy in it. The Chinese garden was at first added to the house as a subsidiary unit but later grew in importance and beauty to become its rival. In some cases the garden even surpasses the house in beauty and in importance. This evolution is not accidental, but the flowering of a civilization which cherishes the ideal of fellowship between nature and man. This understanding is fundamental to our appreciation of the Chinese garden, for without such understanding we might erroneously look upon the garden either as man's effort to bring nature to his feet, or as man's total sinking into insignificance in the face of her grandeur and beauty.

From certain points of view, nature in the Chinese garden may be said to be entirely subordinated to man, for, after all, every attractive structure or colorful flower is primarily meant for man. The garden is a place where he laughs, sings, picks flowers and chases butterflies and pets birds, makes love with maidens and plays with children. Here he spontaneously reveals his nature, the base as well as the noble. Here also he buries his sorrows and difficulties and cherishes his ideals and hopes. It is in the garden that man discovers himself. Indeed he discovers not only his real self but also his ideal self—he returns to his youth. In short, man asserts himself in the garden, and turns it into an area for the expansion of his ego. At least this is the impression one gets from Chinese novels and Chinese paintings. Inevitably the garden is made the scene of man's merriment, escapades, romantic abandonment, spiritual awakening, or the perfection of his finer self.

And yet man in the Chinese garden may be said to be dominated by nature. Here man finds himself outshone by the magnificence of rocks and structures. There is no marble statue to glorify his physical perfection; nor is there any fountain to immortalize his youth. Wherever he stands or sits, he sinks into insignificance, for in the midst of natural splendor and beauty his position can never be impressive. There is no broad stone walk with majestic rows of trees or flowers on the sides to serve as setting for his imposing steps. As a matter of fact, his steps cannot be imposing; on those rugged, zigzag pebble paths he has to walk with humility. He seems to be subordinated to, if not subdued by, nature.

Man and Nature in the Chinese Garden

Such a one-sided observation, however, entirely misses the point. The Chinese never considers himself as opposed or hostile to nature, for if he did, he would either stay inside his house because of fear or he would set out to exploit the Poles just to demonstrate that he can conquer nature. But either attitude is diametrically opposed to the spirit of his civilization. He is taught by his Taoist teachers to be a "companion of nature" and he is counseled by his Confucian sages to "take delight in mountains" and "take delight in rivers." Even the Buddhists, who are disgusted with the world, lure him to the gorgeous and beautiful mountains, where he is promised peace and serenity and joy. So he goes to nature in the spirit of companionship, of enjoyment, and of peace. The garden is simply one of the expressions of this spirit.

How is fellowship of man and nature possible in the garden? The answer lies in the fact that the garden is a harmonious display of the very vitality of both man and nature. This is rhythm, which, to the Chinese, is the highest of all conceivable values, the quintessence of truth, beauty, and goodness of the highest levels of existence. In the realm of philosophy, it is Tao or the Way. In the realm of religion it is the Cosmic Soul. In the realm of art it is Universal Breath. Chinese religion and philosophy become unintelligible as soon as the element of rhythm is removed, for whether spoken of as the Way or Tao, it is at bottom the universal principle of the harmony of the Yin (the female) and the Yang (the male) principles, or the negative and the positive forces of the universe. Underlying all phenomenal and all noumenal existence, there is a spiritual movement running through every aspect of reality. Existence is therefore conceived as a great flow of rhythm, and so is life. The heavens and stars are looked upon as a great symphony, and mountains and rivers, happiness and sorrow, and all the rest, are interpreted in terms of radiation, sequence and alteration.

In art, this rhythmic principle becomes even more conspicuous. Take away rhythm, and Chinese landscape painting immediately collapses as a fine art. It is not a matter of accident or personal idiosyncrasy that the Chinese painters regard rhythmic vitality as the first canon of painting, for movement is the very life of the Chinese pictorial art. Similarly, the beauty and greatness of Chinese music entirely depend on the rhythmic flow of its melody. Instead of a two-dimensional development of harmony and melody, it attempts to create beauty in melody alone. Consequently the rhythmic factors play a greater role in and add more beauty to Chinese music than Western music. Equal emphasis of rhythm may also be found in the Chinese drama, for the Chinese actor sings in rhythm, walks in rhythm, and even moves his eyebrows and swings his sleeves in rhythm. Rhythm in architecture, as you find in the curved roof, is but one expression of the same general spirit, the desire to participate in the great life-flow of the universe.

In the sphere of architecture, the garden is more suitable for the expression of this spirit than any other structure. Almost every part of the garden is rhythmic in expression.

31

CHINESE HOUSES AND GARDENS

The winding walks, the round gates, the zigzag paths, the melody-like walls, the rockeries which are frozen music in themselves, and flowers and trees and birds are all echoes and counterpoints of rhythm. The Chinese in the garden shares this life-flow at every moment and every turn. As he enters the gate of the garden, his body and his soul alike immediately flow with this stream. Here he physically lingers, emotionally wanders, and he hums verses in the evening breeze and sings under the moon. Man and nature together move on. This is why the garden is the ideal scene of romance. This is also why the garden is a most inspiring place for that intense and vigorous mental activity, meditation. The garden is a symphony of rhythm. In it, man and nature together move on.

The skyward direction of this movement culminates in the curved roof of the pavilion. As the curved roof is the characteristic aspect of the pavilion and the dominating feature of the Chinese garden, it is important to find out what the curved roof really means. Western scholars have attempted to explain this peculiar phenomenon by associating it with the tent, asserting that the curve is a frank and direct imitation of it. This theory claims to be realistic and scientific. But it is precisely the scientific test that it fails to stand. For the Chinese are an agricultural people, with no experience of tent life. Furthermore, if the curved roof is the objectification of our memory of the tent, then the more ancient the building, the more should its roof be curved. But, quite to the contrary, the roofs of ancient buildings were not curved. The use of clay and loess bricks in ancient China required the use of straight lines and angles instead of the curve.

A similar theory suggests that the curved roof imitates the contour of a tree. If this is the case, it should be the upward curve of tree branches that captivates the imagination of the Chinese. In Chinese poetry, however, what is glorified is not the upward movement of trees, but the downward movement, as in the case of the weeping willow. In Chinese painting, the conventional outlines of pine branches do resemble the curved roof somewhat, but the characteristic tendency of tree leaves or branches, such as those of the bamboo, the plum, the willow, etc., is definitely downward. Those who think that the Chinese shape their roofs just as they shape their written characters, face the same difficulty, for although the curved roof perfectly resembles the almost circular swing of the downward side-stroke in calligraphy, the characteristic curve in the ancient Chinese script, the seal style, is downward.

The attempt to interpret the curved roof on strictly metaphysical terms is not any happier. To say that the roof embraces heaven while the walls encircle the earth is to confer upon architecture a function entirely alien to it. It is more logical to say that the curved roof reminds us of the flying sparrow; it is a magnificent and impressive presentation of the bird motive. This theory has the support of the fact that the figure of a rooster often adorns the Chinese roof. Yet from a certain point of view, the rooster figure tends to deny rather than affirm the bird motive theory. The rooster figure is the survival of our primitive agricultural life when dogs and fowls shared the roof as well as the interior of our houses. But agricultural life is primarily settled life, and the house is the very symbol of that settled life. People who are settled have no particular love for flying sparrows or soaring eagles.

Other explanations are more true to facts. Since the weight of the tiles in a Chinese building is tremendous, it is natural that trusses are bent and it is a matter of necessity that they are reinforced at the end to lighten pressure. This reinforcement in the form of a heavy mass of timber requires an upward movement to eliminate the feeling of weight. In other words, because of the use of tiles and trusses, the Chinese builders have no choice but to bow to the nature of building materials. Personally I think these explanations carry some truth, but not the whole truth. Faithfulness to the nature of building materials, I think, is the result of something deeper and more significant in Chinese architecture. It is the evidence of something deep in the hearts of the Chinese, which is nothing short of the love for rhythm.

Thus we see that the Chinese garden has a deep esthetic significance to the Chinese. It is a mistake to regard it as a supplement to the house. I am not denying that it does supplement. It does it in more ways than one. Fundamentally it fulfills a need of the Chinese spirit which the house denies. In spite of the presence of dwarf trees and landscape paintings inside the house, the house is completely human in purpose and usage even to the exclusion of nature. From dawn to dusk, the Chinese inside the house lives in the thickness of human relationships and moral discipline, and under the weight and pressure of a mundane existence. His romantic craving for a freer life is suppressed. He has neither the space nor the time for his playful moods. It is in such condition of spiritual bondage that he makes the garden, to fulfill the need of the romantic side of his nature. Therefore the garden may be regarded as a protest against the restriction in the house. We may therefore say that the house and the garden stand in sharp contrast to each other. While the house is a place for man's serious moods, the garden is a place for his playful moments. In the house man is in the society of his fellow beings, but in the garden he is in the society of nature. Inside the house he is a Confucian with all his moral codes, conventions, and a prescribed way of life, whereas in the garden he is a Taoist, a romantic, primitivistic, care-free "new-born child."

But the garden is more than a supplement to the house. It fulfills a higher function of life, the function that only art can fulfill. It is not sentimentalism that the Chinese looks upon the garden as a form of art. Since it serves as a release of man's suppressed nature, it offers him refuge. In this sense, the Chinese garden, like other forms of art, is a place for escape. At the same time, through the beauty, purity, refinement and nobility of nature, it serves as a purgation of man's passions. It is here that man becomes natural, spontaneous, and sincere. Furthermore, when a person enters the garden, he enters a realm

33

of ideal existence, a dreamland, and a wonderland where he may look through the glass window to catch a glimpse of what reality is like. He is here at home with nature.

It is a mistake to regard the Chinese garden as mere decoration. True, it is decorative. All the decorative elements of Chinese architecture are found there. There are pagodas and pavilions. There are mountains and rocks. There are a host of symbols in different forms and shapes. As in any other Chinese structure, the walls and columns and doors and windows are richly ornamented, with brilliant colors in gold and red, with scenes of romance and inscriptions of classical poetry. But the Chinese soon realizes that color and form are but mere superficialities. Therefore, in architecture as in painting, he goes beyond the decorative elements to seek the higher beauty of art.

As I have said, the garden fulfills a higher function than merely supplementing the house or decorating it. It offers an appropriate background for the spontaneous flow of man's spirit, for esthetically the garden is a most suitable place for man's spiritual emancipation. It is an outstanding characteristic of Chinese architecture that instead of being overburdened with weight, mass, and matter, it overcomes them all. The Chinese building is primarily built of wood. Where stone is necessary, it is made to look like wood. The oppressive dome is eliminated. Trusses and columns all appear simple and light. The effect of lightness is accentuated with the gentle flow of rhythm. The result is that matter is entirely subdued in favor of the free expression of the spirit. And yet, formalism and regularity necessarily prevail in a building, for the rectangle remains the basis of design and the whole structure develops around an axial plan. Symmetry and the straight line cannot be avoided. The human spirit, therefore, inevitably bows to formalism and regularity. Insofar as it submits to such restraint, its freedom is restricted.

Formalism and regularity, on the other hand, entirely disappear from the garden. The keynote of arrangements, whether of rockeries, gates, paths, or flower beds, is irregularity. Formality is sacrificed in favor of informality. Both the straight line and the sharp corner are dispensed with, to such a degree that the entire garden becomes a diffusion of curves. Gates and windows, which by nature lend themselves to the formal treatment of straight lines and angles, here stand in the shape of a leaf, a flower vase, or the moon. Even the column and the wall, the regularity of which is unavoidable because straight lines cannot be eliminated, are made irregular by luxurious decoration, plastering, and carving, so that the vertical column and the horizontal wall are overshadowed by irregular designs. Geometric arrangements are abhorred because both the geometric pattern of thought and the geometric pattern of life limit the freedom of the spirit. By rejecting the geometric pattern, by using the curve instead of the straight line, and by eliminating the weight and mass of matter, the garden is made the cradle of freedom for the spirit.

This freedom is not to be conceived as careless, orderless, irresponsible activity. It is freedom within a prescribed order. Nature is never looked upon by the Chinese as chaotic or disorganized. Heaven and earth co-exist in harmony, and the four seasons run their course regularly. Thus the Confucians and the Taoists unite in reminding the Chinese that there is a universal principle pervading all things, whether in the realm of physical nature or in the sphere of human life. This universal principle expresses itself in two aspects, the Yin and the Yang, or the negative and the positive forces. In casting away regularity in favor of irregularity for his garden, the Chinese never violates the regularity of nature. Natural order is religiously preserved. For example, miniature rock mountains are never built to the exclusion of a stream or a water-fall, just as in Chinese landscape painting, mountain and water never appear one without the other. For it is the order of nature that mountain and water co-exist, one representing the positive principle and the other the negative principle of the universe. Representative flowers of the four seasons must rule in the realm of time. Hedges might not be trimmed. Grass might not be mowed. And yet harmony prevails over all the apparently wild and rustic. Over and above irregularity and informality, there reigns a higher order, the order of nature.

In thus establishing the order of nature in the garden, man really re-creates nature. The garden remains a galaxy of flowers and birds and rocks and stones. But nature here does not appear wild or chaotic. Order is restored and harmony is never disturbed. While rockeries and stone mosaics everywhere remind us of the grandeur of nature, they remind us at the same time of the genius of man. For nature is reconstructed, beautified, and idealized by him. In this process of re-creation, neither does he allow himself to dominate nature, nor does he allow himself to be dominated. Any massive structure is eliminated from the garden, like the dome, the massive roof, the imposing arch, or a great body of water. To avoid the feeling of oppression by nature, weight is minimized, by accentuating the curve of the bridge, by opening more doors and windows in the wall, by bending the stone walk, by diffusively ornamenting the column, by minifying the rockeries, by making stone look like wood, and by shunning massive trees. Yet at the same time, all the elegance and grace and beauty one finds in the garden are those of nature, which the elegance and grace and beauty of man never attempt to outshine or even to rival.

This harmony of man and nature in the flow of the great stream of rhythm makes the Chinese garden more than something merely secular. It is true that no one would look upon the Chinese garden as a religious structure. The Chinese have a god for the house, one for the kitchen, one for the door, and one even for the chicken house, but no god for the garden. The pagoda, originally a religious edifice in India, is used in China not only as a mausoleum for some relics of the Buddha, but also as decoration. When it is used in the garden, particularly as a part of rockeries, it becomes a decorative element pure and simple. Other structures face the south, whereas the garden is not bound by such convention. But in spite of all this, we cannot deny the fact that the garden is regarded as an ideal place for meditation. Meditation may be purely moral, an effort at self-introspection.

35

Intense and sincere meditation, however, inevitably leads to the absorption in the Infinite.

Furthermore, the Primeval Pair of the Yin and Yang, of the male and the female forces, the active and the passive principles, are faithfully represented in hills and ponds, in stones and woods, and remind us of the harmony and order of the universe. The five elements of metal, wood, water, fire, and earth are deeply religious to the Chinese because they unite all forms of existence into a network of correspondences so that thunder, wind, rain, air, and cloud have direct correspondence with the five directions which in turn act on the five mentals, the five colors, the five organs of the human body and all other mentionable phenomena. These five elements have their symbolism in the Oriental garden, particularly the Japanese, where the element of earth is represented in hills and islands, that of water in ponds and waterfalls, that of fire in glowing flowers, that of wood in trees, that of wind in the power which swings tree branches and scatters flower petals, and that of metal in stones. The Infinite and the finite are at every instance correlated. It is in this most fundamental sense that in the Chinese garden man and nature become one.

The Chinese Love of Home and Symbolism

By Shao Chang Lee

FOR centuries the Chinese people have been taught by their sages to seek real pleasure and enjoyment at home. The home may be nothing but a cave dwelling, a mere shack, a mud hut; nevertheless it can be transformed into a little bit of heaven on earth, for in it live one's parents, brothers, sisters, wife, and children, and around it are the distant hills, the nearby brooks, and all the wonderful things that nature has produced for the good of mankind. To the sages it is the Will of Heaven that the home should be the true abode of affection, peace, and rest, where harmonious relationships not only between man and man but also between man and nature are to be cultivated and the five blessings of life are to be enjoyed. [According to the *Book of History* (Shu Ching) the five blessings of life are: (1) long life, (2) riches, (3) good health and peace of mind, (4) love of virtue, and (5) an end fulfilling the Will of Heaven.]

Approximately three-fourths of the Chinese people engage in agriculture. Daily they toil to make their fields fertile and fruitful and their gardens useful and soul-satisfying. As they toil, they learn to be happy with their work and to enjoy the beauty of nature as did the ancient worthies who sang:

When the sun rises, I toil;
When the sun sets, I rest.
I dig wells for water;
I till the fields for food.
What has the power of the king to do with me?

I pluck chrysanthemums on the eastern hedge,
Then lifting my eyes, I gaze long at the Southern Hill.
The mountain air is fresh at dawn and at dusk;
The flying birds circle back and forth in pairs.
In these things there lies a deep meaning;
Yet when I wish to express it, I forget the words.

I planted beans at the foot of the Southern Hill.
Grasses grew and so the bean sprouts are sparse.
Early I rise to pluck the weeds and till the field.
At night I return, carrying on my back the moon and the hoe.
The road is narrow and the bushes are thick and tall.
Dew drops dampen my clothing.
Though my coat is wet, I do not regret it.
My hope is that my wish will not be unfruitful.

At times the Chinese people have to struggle with pernicious forces which threaten to destroy their homes, fields, and gardens. But often the struggle to them is a blessing in disguise, for during the period of suffering there develop in them those elements of character which make them "the world's best agriculturists: industry and thrift, the ability to enlist every source of help, and the endurance to begin patiently afresh when destruction seemed well-nigh inevitable." (J. G. Anderson, in *Children of the Yellow Earth*, p. 144.) And "when the times of violence and disorder are over, when all is peaceful and calm" again, they set out their dishes and meat stands and drink to one another's happiness. They sing again the ancient song:

With mass of gorgeous flowers
The cherry trees are crowned,
But none within this world of ours
Like brothers can be found . . .

Brothers indoors may fight;
But insults from without
Join them at once, and they unite
The common foe to rout . . .

Children and wife we love;
Union with them is sweet
As lute's soft strain that soothes our pain.
How joyous do we meet!

We brothers, old and young,
Gladly do our own part;
For our accord does peace afford
And lasting joy impart. . . . *

The Chinese people love dearly their homes, fields, and gardens, and they often make attempts to express their feeling by pictures or words. If they are unable to draw or if words fail them, then they recite the poems of T'ao Yuan-ming, whom Lin Yutang considers "the most harmonious product of Chinese culture." T'ao Yuan-ming, says Lin Yutang, is "a perfect example of the true lover of life, because in him the rebellion against worldly desires did not lead him to attempt a total escape, but has reached a harmony with the life of the senses." (Lin Yutang, *The Importance of Living*, pp. 115-121.) In a series of six poems entitled "Back to My Garden Home," T'ao Yuan-ming described his home and environment. The first poem runs as follows:

Since my youth I have been out of tune with the multitude;
To love the hills and mountains is my nature.
But by mistake I fell into vulgar ways,
And for thirty years I was astray.

---

* A translation of an ancient ballad after that of James Legge. See Legge's *The Book of Poetry* (republished by the Chinese Book Company, Shanghai), pp. 187-8. Compare Arthur Waley's version in his *The Book of Songs*, pp. 203-4.

A captive bird longs for the old woods,
A fish in the tank for its familiar pool.
Long was I kept in a cage,
But now . . . free at last . . . I have returned to Nature's ways.

I have cleared the wildland on the southern horizon.
I have built eight or nine grass huts.
Elms and willows shadow the eaves;
Peach and plum trees give shade at my front door.

I see in the distance, as in a haze, the haunts of men;
The lazy smoke lingers over the village.
Dogs bark in the deep lanes;
Cocks crow on top of the mulberry tree . . .

There is no dust, and no clamoring in my courtyard.
*In my empty rooms I enjoy leisurely the idle hours.**

This poem and the one called "Homeward Bound" are on the lips of every school boy and girl. In "Homeward Bound" T'ao Yuan-ming painted word-pictures showing his journey home, his arrival at his home, his garden and field, and the surrounding landscape. This one depicts the poet in his garden:

Daily I wander pleasantly in my garden.
There is a gate, but it is always closed.
I lean on my bamboo cane as I wander about or sit down to rest.
Now and then I raise my head and look at the sky.
The clouds drift from their mountain recesses;
The birds, weary of flying, return to their nests.
Now it is getting dark, and the lovely scene is vanishing;
Still I like to linger beneath the lonely pine.

The rest of the poem tells us more of how T'ao Yuan-ming spent his days at home. He enjoyed sweet conversation with his kin and dispelled his sorrow with his lute and his books. When springtime came he joined other farmers to work in the western fields. Some bright mornings he worked alone, weeding his garden. Sometimes he climbed the Eastern Hill and whistled a tune, or sat beside the limpid stream and penned a verse. Thus he lived till the end, when, without any doubt in his mind, he followed gladly the Will of Heaven.

Such was the simple life of T'ao Yuan-ming, who made his home truly an abode of affection, peace, and rest. As Lin Yutang has said, "He remains today a beacon shining through the ages, forever a symbol to the lesser poets and writers of what the highest human character should be."

The life of T'ao Yuan-ming has been an inspiration not only to the poets and writers of later periods of Chinese literature, but also to the painters, especially to land-

---

* Compare Arthur Waley's version of the same poem in his *170 Chinese Poems*, p. 113.

scape painters. Artists often select lines from his romantic picture-poems as themes for their compositions. Like him they let their gaze rest on the autumn clouds and their souls soar high. They sing in the pavilions and towers in praise of the spring breeze that playfully flutters their flowing gowns. At day's end they return home to their studios. There, with brushes in hand, they swiftly transfer to silk or paper scrolls the splendor of nature and the loveliness of man's handiwork. Their landscape paintings are not intended to be literal representations of the surface view of nature but are poetic interpretations of nature's mystic meaning. In a large scroll of this kind one may see a magnificent landscape actually including all these: mountain peaks, quaint rocks, turbulent cascades, green forests, tall pine trees, willow trees, winds, mists, winding roads, distant temples, streams, bridges, pavilions, and rustic houses. Figures representing sages like T'ao Yuan-ming may be seen walking over a bridge or standing before a distant waterfall, followed by boys carrying lutes, or bundles of books or sprays of blossoms. The whole scene is one of serenity of the air and harmony of the world of nature. As one looks at such a picture, one's imagination is aroused almost to envy: one wishes to be in the scene.

In these poetic and imaginative paintings a noted master of pictorial art and an expert landscape architect of the seventeenth century named Chi Ch'eng discovered the principles of harmony, irregularity, concealment, suggestion, and surprise, which he later applied in the building of garden homes for two retired officials of his time. (Chi Ch'eng was a native of Sungling, near Soochow. He built garden homes for the Honorable Wu You-yu in Chinling and the Honorable Wang Shih-heng in Luankiang.) In 1635 Chi Ch'eng published a book on landscape gardening, to which his friend Tsao Yuan-fu of Kushu gave the title *Yuan Yeh*, for it showed the creative power of the author, his mastery of the subject, and his enthusiasm for garden art. Furthermore, it was the first book of its kind in the Chinese world of literature. In it Chi Ch'eng recorded the principles of garden making. One of the points he emphasized was: "Make the garden like a landscape painting." This phrase has become a maxim and we see today that a typical Chinese garden is "indeed a landscape painting in three dimensions." Chi Ch'eng's book has not been translated into any of the European languages . . . partly because of the difficulty of rendering his flowery language into any other tongue. In it he discussed the following topics: (1) the selection of ground-plot; (2) the laying of foundations for the reception hall, the archway, the view-tower, the study room, the pavilion, the corridor, and the rockery; (3) the construction of the various buildings: the use and the symbolism of each building; (4) exterior decorations: the designs for gates, doors, windows, corridors, and balustrades; (5) lattice patterns; (6) the construction of walls: the kinds of walls; (7) pavement: the use of pebbles, broken tiles, chips of stone, and fragments of porcelain for the construction; patterns for pavements; (8) the creation of a wild landscape with peaks, cliffs, streams, and waterfalls; and (9) the selection of rocks for the rockery.

The Chinese Love of Home and Symbolism

The gardens which Chi Ch'eng built filled his patrons with an inexpressible delight. That is what all gardens should do. A garden which delights, charms, inspires, and gives lasting pleasure to its owner and those who visit it, is itself a bit of nature, an earthly paradise wherein the man of understanding freely roams and serenely contemplates the good, the true, the beautiful, the infinite.

When we enter a Chinese garden we find ourselves surrounded with symbols. The shape of the door, the design of the window grille, the decorations, the trees and flowers are symbols, whether or not one recognizes them as such. The significance of symbols has long been appreciated by the Chinese* and they would agree with Thomas Carlyle, when he said: "The Universe is but one vast Symbol of God; nay, if thou will have it, what is man himself, but a symbol of God; is not all he does symbolical? . . . It is in and through symbols that man, consciously or unconsciously, lives, moves, works, and has his being . . ."

Here is a gate in the shape of a moon, which many Occidental visitors call "the moon gate." It may represent the moon in its full glory, but its round shape suggests the idea of perfection and reminds one of the saying of an ancient sage, "Be round without, but be square within" (*Wei yuan erh nei fang*), which amounts to saying, "Be smooth, but be a square shooter." And over there is a doorway made in the form of a vase. Its symbolic function is to convey the idea of peace, for in Chinese the word *vase* has the same sound as the word for the word *peace*; both are pronounced "ping." As one walks through such a doorway one seems to hear the benediction: *Ch'u ju ping an*, meaning "May peace be with thee in thy coming in and thy going out."

The symbolism of the designs of the window grilles is concerned chiefly with such blessings as *fu, lo,* and *shou*—happiness, abundance, and long life. Its beauty can be readily appreciated for it not only expresses one's worldly desires but also satisfies one's esthetic longings. (See the excellent work *A Grammar of Chinese Lattice* by Daniel Sheets Dye, published in two volumes by the Harvard University Press, 1937.)

Among the decorative designs are the *lung* (dragon), the *feng huang* (the Chinese bird of paradise), the deer, the crane, and the bat. The *lung* is a fabulous animal created by the ancient myth-makers to represent the idea of power and change. It is an assemblage of several animal forms: it has "the head of a camel, the horns of a deer, the ears of an ox, the eyes of a hare, the body of a snake covered with the scales of a carp, the claws of an eagle, and the paws of a tiger." It is considered to be a divine, benevolent creature with power to make itself visible or invisible at will and to create clouds and to bring

* See Z. D. Sung's *The Symbols of Yi King* and *The Texts of Yi King*, published by The China Modern Education Co., Shanghai, 1934 and 1935 respectively. See also *Outlines of Chinese Symbolism and Art Motives* by C. A. S. Williams, published by Kelly and Walsh, Shanghai, 1932.

rain to the farmers. It is seen coiling around columns, lying on roofs, adorning balustrades and walls.

The *feng huang*, miscalled "phoenix," is the Chinese bird of paradise. It is not the sacred bird of Egyptian mythology that burns itself on the altar and rises again from the ashes young and beautiful. It is not an emblem of resurrection. According to Chinese legend, the *feng huang*, like the *lung* or dragon, is a divine, benevolent creature; it lives in the "Vermillion Cave, feeds itself on bamboo-shoots, and drinks from the Sweet Spring." Its body is adorned with five colors and bears five signs for virtue, benevolence, justice, faithfulness, and wisdom. It symbolizes queenly virtue, feminine grace, love, and happy marriage.

The deer is a symbol of abundance and long life. It holds in its mouth the sacred fungus of immortality. The crane, being a very long-lived creature, symbolizes longevity, and is generally depicted under a pine tree or beside a branch of plum blossoms. The bat is an emblem of general blessing, because the word *bat* in Chinese has the same sound as the word for *blessing*. Furthermore, there is a kind of bat which eats mosquitoes, flies, and other insect pests and is a most helpful ally of the farmers. A *fu* (bat) to the farmers is a *fu* (blessing) indeed.

From a myriad variety of flowers procurable for the gardens, the Chinese select a few. In spring they have the peony flowers, the peach blossoms, and the plum blossoms. The peony, regarded as the "king of flowers," symbolizes wealth and honor. The peach and plum blossoms symbolize physical charm and the loveliness of women as well as the spirit of "the quiet, poor scholar." In summer there are the orchids, the magnolias, the pomegranate, and the lotus. The orchid is called "the favorite of the kings," and is used to symbolize culture, refinement, and nobility of character. The magnolia suggests the "fragrance of virtue," while the pomegranate represents fecundity. The lotus is an emblem of truth and purity. In a short essay on "Why I love the Lotus," Chou Tun-i, a distinguished philosopher of the eleventh century, wrote: "How stainless it rises from its slimy bed! How modestly it reposes on the clear pool! Symmetrically perfect. Its subtle perfume is wafted far and wide; while there it rests in spotless state, something to be regarded reverently from a distance, and not to be profaned by familiar approach." The important flower of the autumn is the chrysanthemum, the favorite of T'ao Yuan-ming. It is a symbol of gentility, good fellowship, and longevity. In winter there is the gardenia, the symbol of graceful charm. On New Year Day there is the narcissus, the symbol of good fortune.

The trees which the Chinese people love to plant in their gardens are the willows, the pines, the peach, the plum, and the bamboo. These trees are as common as humanity, but they are as admirable as the highest type of statesmen, clergymen, and artists, and they are used to symbolize those qualities which enrich life. The willow represents grace, for its tender and slender branches wave as easily, as elegantly, and as rhythmically as the sleeves of a dancing girl. It also represents the sentiment of friendship. In olden times it was customary to pluck a branch of willow and give it to a departing friend. It is a symbol of purity and mercy. Kuan-yin, the Goddess of Mercy, is said to use willow branches only when she sprinkles the water of life upon the sick and dying to purify and revive them. The pine tree symbolizes the robustness, dignity, and majesty of a wise old man; it shows how to grow old gracefully. It also denotes integrity and the power to withstand the whips of adversity. The peach and plum trees represent brotherliness and cordial relationships, and symbolize the promising pupils of a worthy teacher. The bamboo tree, with its tall and slender stalks and its long and narrow leaves, is always a favorite of scholars and artists. It symbolizes virtues such as fidelity, constancy, humility, wisdom, and gentleness. Because the older it grows the stronger it becomes, it is an emblem of healthy long life. It is very much enjoyed "in the intimacy of a scholar's home" and very much used as an art motif by the poet-painters.

The beauty and usefulness of the Chinese flowers and trees are more and more appreciated by Occidental people though their symbolism is difficult to understand. Ernest H. Wilson, an American naturalist, enthusiastically called China "The Mother of Gardens." He wrote: "China is, indeed, the Mother of Gardens, for of the countries to which our gardens are most deeply indebted she holds the foremost place. From the bursting into blossoms of the Forsythias and Yulan Magnolias in the early spring to the Peonies and Roses in summer and the Chrysanthemums in the autumn, China's contributions to the floral wealth of gardens is in evidence."

In sum, it may be said that everything in a Chinese garden appears to have been spiritualized and seems to have an inner meaning. Pine, bamboo, and plum trees are affectionately called "the Three Friends of Winter," and the plum blossom, the orchid, the chrysanthemum and the pine tree are fancifully personified as "the Four Princely Scholars." Even a rock has a personality. Mi Fei, a renowned artist of the Sung Dynasty, once addressed a quaint rock as his "Big Brother," and Ko Chiu-ssu, a painter of the Yuan period, bowed reverently before a majestic rock as his friend. This is not a remnant of stone-worship. It is an evidence of the power of the Zen Buddhists, who preached that the heart of the universe is Buddha and that "the Buddha heart" is in all nature. The Zen Buddhists chant thus:

> *The golden light upon the sunlit peaks,*
> *The water murmuring in the pebbly creeks*
> *Are Buddha! In the stillness, hark, He speaks!*

The name of a garden as well as the names of everything therein are symbolical. Take, for example, the name of the Summer Palace near Peiping. It is known as *I Ho Yuan,* meaning "Garden of Harmony and Longevity." What a beautiful name! When its inner meaning is sensed the beauty of the whole garden is enhanced a hundredfold.

43

Chinese Houses and Gardens

Eleven centuries ago Liu Yu-shih, a farmer and scholar, recorded the inner meaning of his garden home somewhat as follows:

A mountain is famed not for its height
but for its being the abode of immortals.
A pool is renowned not for its depth
but for its being the home of the dragon.
Humble indeed is this house of mine
But it is filled with the fragrance of virtue.
The mossy veins of the stone steps are green;
The color of the grass gleams through the screen.
Here we have chats and laughter with eminent scholars;
There is no stupid person passing through.
Here we may play on the simple lute
Or read the Diamond Sutra.
There are no noisy musical instruments to confound our ears,
And no official dispatches to weary our beings.
This is like the home of Chuko at Nanyang
Or the pavilion of Tzuyun in far west Szechuan.
Confucius said:
In the dwelling of a true gentleman,
what unrefinement can there be?

Indeed, in the dwelling of a true gentleman, what unrefinement can there be?

Part Two: Plates

Corner of a private garden in Nantao, native city of Shanghai. Note the interesting shape of the door and wall.

Entrance in the shape of a cherry blossom. Note the fantastic shape of the rockery. Sign above the entrance reads, "T'an Yu," meaning, "To Seek the Mysterious."

A hexagonal doorway leading to a courtyard. Sign above the doorway reads, "The place to cultivate the friendship of the moon."

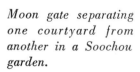

Moon gate separating one courtyard from another in a Soochou garden.

This cobbled walk bordered with sedge leads through a gateway that gives an unusual sense of transition. One enters through a moon-shaped frame, and two steps further emerges from a rectangular doorway.

The moon-shaped gateway leading to an inner court is enhanced by a curved arbor for vines, in this Hangchow garden. Note the low seat on the side.

Unusual doorway in the shape of a Chinese candle.

Two doorways of different designs leading to two different courtyards.

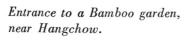

Entrance to a Bamboo garden, near Hangchow.

A doorway in the shape of a Ming jar, leading into a rock-garden.

Entrance to a monastery garden near Hangchow. Ming Dynasty.

Private residence in Hangchow, built during the Ming Dynasty, 1368-1644. Inscription above the moon gate reads, "The path and the bamboo lead one to the place of mystery."

Situated in the center of a large garden, this little white stucco building provides a shady resting place. Note the fretwork window and the unusual shape of the doorway.

Simple but very artistic doorway in an old Chinese garden at Nantao.

A gate with classical lines contrasting with the interesting fresco above. The Chinese inscription reads, "The fragrance of antiquity lasts forever."

Entrance to the great stadium of Shanghai. The design over the doorway is a modern adaptation from the Peiping Imperial Palace.

Narrow passageway connecting various rooms of an old residence.

Vase shaped doorway from an old private garden, near Shanghai.

If the moon gate is built within the house, an open-work door of this design is generally used. Inscription above the gate reads, "The fragrance of all flowers penetrates the clouds." Inscription on the left panel reads, "The moon shines upon the wavelets."

These tall temple doors have no hinges, but swing on dowel pins at top and bottom. When open, these doors cause the interior of the temple to seem one with the open courtyard. When they are closed, the open-work carving admits a dim screened light. Temple in Hangchow, built during the Ming Dynasty.

This unique doorway of lacquered teak wood is one of several entrances into the house from the courtyard. Private residence in Shanghai.

59

A well balanced courtyard with the ever-present moon gate.

Another example of a doorway. The Sung inscription above reads, "Quiet Grove."

A doorway in the shape of a Ming vase leading into an inner courtyard.

The old Chinese artists abhorred monotony and in designing doorways often gave their imagination free reign.

61

This octagonal doorway is typical of many in China. Private residence in Nantao. The inscription above the doorway reads, "Linger and enjoy."

Present-day China makes modern materials conform to traditional architecture. Steel and concrete make the walls for this Hangchow restaurant.

A gateway frames a fall landscape near Hangchow.

A Fifteenth Century pavilion seen through the vase-shaped window of a residence in Sungkiang.

Square glazed tiles in a narrow molded frame form a window grille in a native Shanghai residence.

Pierced pink stucco walls and glazed tile roof form this tea pavilion of the late Ming Dynasty.

Corner of a courtyard, Yuan Dynasty, 1280-1368. Though different in design, one grille harmonizes well with the other.

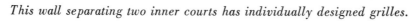

This wall separating two inner courts has individually designed grilles.

An interesting bit of Chinese garden architecture. Note the graceful curve of the wall, the simple design of the open-work windows, and the skillful arrangement of trees and flowers. Built during the late Ming Dynasty. Sungkiang, near Shanghai.

Portion of a Soochow garden. Note the informality of vines and foliage; the well-balanced design of the windows.

Longevity is symbolized in this Ming window.

Chinese inner garden of well balanced design, with an unusual open-work window. The slanted railing serves as the rest for a long seat.

Side view of an old Chinese villa. The artistry of man is effectively enhanced by a slight touch of the handiwork of Nature.

An exquisite temple window in Hangchow with Feng-huang bird design, delicately carved and tinted in pastel colors, unglazed. A rare specimen beautifully executed.

Intricate design and interesting symbolism. The window of five blessings —long life, riches, good health and peace of mind, love of virtue, and an end fulfilling the Will of Heaven.

Dragon design, companion to window on opposite page.

It seems incredible that this fragile filigree is made of clay. Designed by an unknown artist early in the Seventeenth Century. Soochow.

Window, shaped after "the peach of longevity." Sungkiang, near Shanghai.

An ornamental vase-shaped window, with lotus blossoms and leaves in bas-relief above on the wall. Ch'ien Lung period, 1736-1796. In a private residence, Soochow.

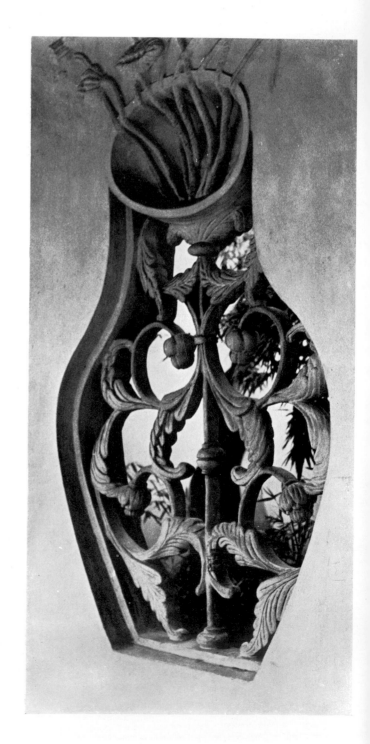

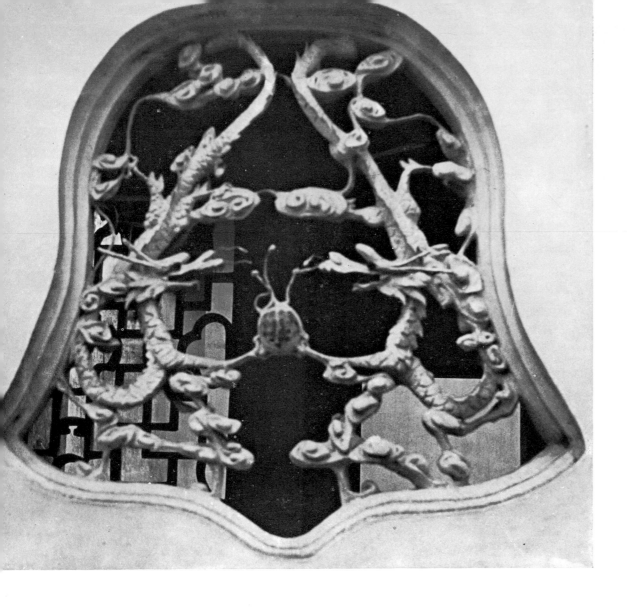

From the Ch'ien Lung period comes this ornamental bell-shaped window with embossed design of dragons.

Window in the shape of a fan with designs of pine tree, crane and fungi.

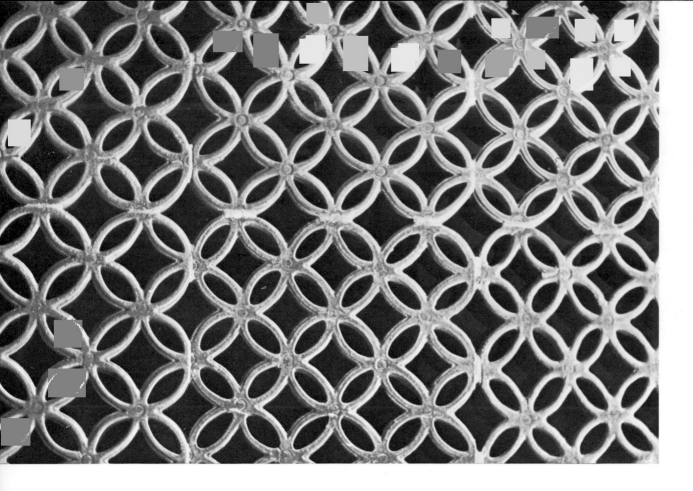

Common roof tiles make an interesting pattern in grilles of late Ming Dynasty.

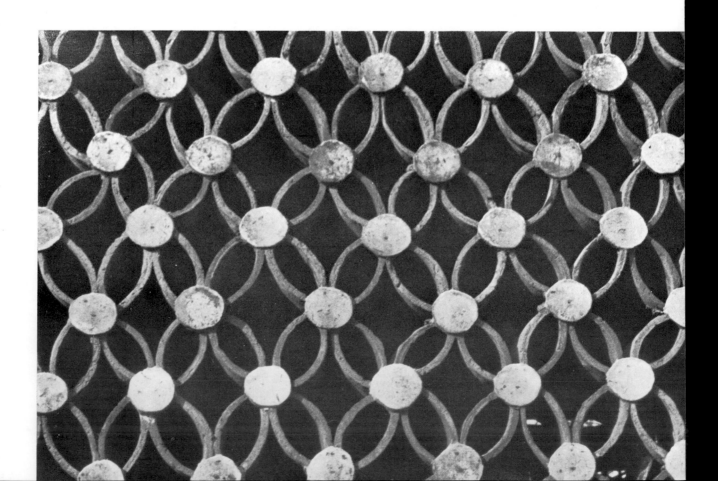

The Feng-huang bird (Phoenix), a grille in natural dark gray clay, unglazed, made over three hundred years ago.

Molded clay window of simple design.

A moon-shaped window with designs of pine, bamboo and plum blossom, symbolizing enduring friendship.

Two more examples of clay grille work.

Window in Shanghai Public Library, showing ancient design in modern architecture.

Bamboo lace through a filigree of clay. In a private residence, Soochow.

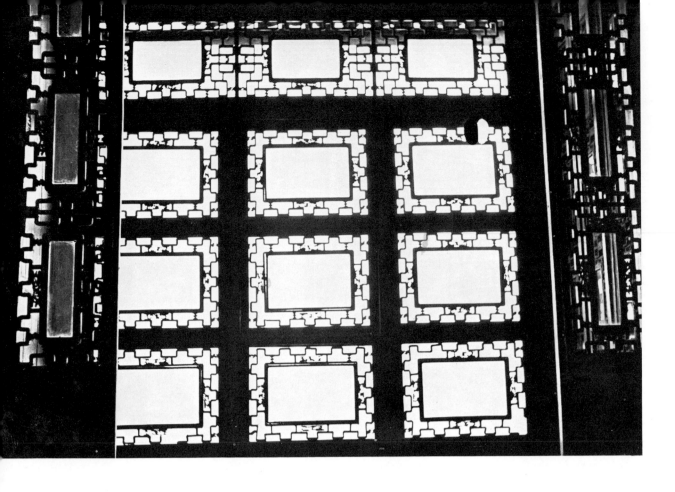

Chinese windows in silhouette.

Interior of a dining room. Note the peculiar Chinese arrangement of teakwood furniture in front of the windows.

Reception room of a Chinese home, Hangchow. Teakwood furniture inlaid with marble, rare porcelain bowl and delicate carvings above doorway.

Interior view of a famous Hangchow residence. An open-work moon gate separates the drawing room into two sections. Rare teakwood and lacquer furniture with pots of chrysanthemums on stands combine to give the pleasing appearance.

*Corner of reception room in a Hangchow villa, with scrolls of Ming paintings,
framed ideographs by famous calligraphists on the walls, and fantastic rocks
on a teakwood marble-top table.*

Seated on this magnificent carved teakwood throne, the Empress Dowager Tzu Hsi (1860-1908) formally received her guests and visitors in the Summer Palace at Peiping. The teakwood table has the same masterful and intricate carving as the throne, and both are set off to advantage by the bright lacquer screen behind. On panels of imperial yellow are figures of vases. All are inlaid with exquisite jade, carnelian, amber, rose quartz, amethyst, mother-of-pearl, crystal and green quartz. On either side are the royal fans of peacock feathers mounted in gold and silver frames, with teakwood handles.

Rich yellow brocade curtains the bed of the Empress Dowager Tzu Hsi in the Summer Palace at Peiping. Now open to the public, this carefully guarded room has perhaps never before been photographed. The imperial yellow drapes, bedspread and cushions are profusely embroidered with dragons—symbol of majesty. Seated beside the low bed table of carved teak, the Empress Dowager enjoyed her tea in the daytime. The arm chair, obviously of Western manufacture, lends a sharp note of contrast, which, however, has been somewhat softened by a cover of tasseled Chinese embroidery.

A Chinese ancestral hall. Dignified by two stately marble pillars and four teakwood columns. Some twenty-five feet in height. These two-hundred-year-old columns, some round, some fluted, were carved, pediment and all, from single blocks of marble. Chung Shan District, Canton.

A corner of the "Dragon Cave Temple" near Hangchow. The arched tile ceiling is supported by beautifully carved teakwood beams and square granite columns inscribed with artistic ideographs.

A group of highly prized petrified logs placed behind a rockery of carefully fitted, unhewn rock. Note the typical concave arched roof lines. Private garden in West Lake, Hangchow.

A portion of a rock garden and balustrade. In a private residence near Shanghai's native city.

The simple dignity of a stone bench makes a striking contrast with the grotesque little mountain and its goblin cave leading down to a lower terrace.

This walk in a private garden leads past a tantalizing rockery typical of the Chinese love for fantasy expressed in stone.

Through the windows and doorways of this graceful pavilion one gets a glimpse of the disarray that makes a Chinese garden so fascinating. Private garden in Soochow.

A view of a garden at West Lake, Hangchow, showing an interesting two-story pavilion constructed upon a base of rocks carefully fitted together.

This private residence near Hangchow is a fine example of Chinese house and garden planning. The walks are never straight but winding and twisting. The traditional rockwork is pierced by trees. This garden was built during the early Ming Dynasty, A. D. 1368-1644.

Trees in autumn color reflected in the still lake at the famous public garden at West Lake, Hangchow.

For four centuries this secluded monastery garden has served as a place of meditation for priests and monks. Built over a tiny spring-fed lake, the temple has a railing which also serves as a back to the long bench on the garden side.

This pavilion with its sturdy, yet graceful railing has survived through several centuries. West Lake, Hangchow.

This octagonal pavilion is built at the center of an artificial lake and is connected by stone causeways to the shore. Note the design on each section of the railing. Private garden in Soochow.

Arched bridges and winding paths lead the visitors to this Wang garden, near Shanghai.

This little lakeside pavilion is a masterpiece of design. Half enclosed, it still preserves balance by means of a skillfully wrought moon window. Its harmonious combination of a lake-fronting porch with a sheltered portion typifies the Chinese mastery of functional design, unified by creative artistry. Built during the early Yuan Dynasty.

The joy of boating inspired the designer of this tea house. Reminiscent of a river junk, this craft of brick and tile lies at anchor in the artificial lake created for it. Private garden in Sungkiang.

To enjoy one's tea in serene surroundings this little pavilion was built on the shores of a tiny lake.

A tea house in the shape of a boat, built of brick and marble during the Seventeenth Century. Private garden near Shanghai.

This tea pavilion rests on a man-made island of rock. The openwork of the roof, the eaves and the railing give the whole structure a fragile, fairy-like appearance. Even the pine tree pruned to the shape of a pagoda adds to the delicate atmosphere of the garden. West Lake, near Hangchow. Of recent origin.

Pavilion on a rocky platform. It is not accident that Chinese buildings so often seem to fit into the landscape. The site is always selected with great care not for prominence but rather to form a harmonious and artistic entity with nature.

Tea house of contemporary, less ornate design. Wong's garden, Shanghai.

Rockery and snow-white marble figures of the Eight Immortals, the gods of long life, honor and wealth. Foo dogs and goldfish bowls flank the granite platform.

A rock sentinel and a sun dial grace the entrance to a tea house.

Suggestive of western medieval garden furniture, this granite bench displays an economy of design betraying the skill of the artist. The designer of this garden has blended gracefully the dragon roofed wall and natural boulders into one harmonious composition.

Snow-white marble railings delicately carved.

The famous five-dragon arbors of Pei-hai Park, Peiping, may be seen in the distance.

A low wall around the terrace protects the household on rainy days from dripping roofs and trees. The angular lines and symmetrically placed columns tend to give a classical feeling.

Fine example of Chinese garden architecture—the walks are always winding and twisting . . . never straight. Note the walls and windows gracefully follow the contour of the walk.

An entrance to a private garden, near Shanghai.

An uncommon mode of decoration is this use of lattice work around the courtyard. One of a series, this patio with its many marble tables and pottery seats is a place for serving tea and entertaining guests.

An ancient stone slab forms the top of a contemporary table. The seats are peacock-blue glazed pottery. Private residence in Hangchow.

The noteworthy feature of this table is not the design of the teakwood legs or frame, but the use of the great brick for the top. It is one of the massive slabs with which the audience hall of an ancient Imperial Palace was once paved. The carved marble seats, as well as the frame of the table, are of recent origin. Private residence in Soochow.

Of exquisite taste is the design of this garden furniture. The simplicity and grace of line belie the massiveness of the granite from which this table and seats were hewn.

This massive furniture of granite displays a graceful symmetry. Note the originality of design in the use of bricks for the floor.

Confucius: The wise find pleasure in water; the virtuous find pleasure in hills.

Some chinese artists of long ago found pleasure in creating these grotesque dragon heads, the lower one almost reminiscent of Aztec sculpture.

Ancient fountain-heads near Hangchow— serving both artistic and utilitarian purposes.

A modern version in front of the Municipal Museum of Greater Shanghai.

102

In one of Europe's ancient cathedrals this might well be a baptismal font. The Chinese sculptor intended it for a bird bath, using as his inspiration the lotus flower, symbol of purity and loveliness. Of a coarse granite, early Ming Dynasty, it stood, until the Sino-Japanese war of 1937, in the courtyard of a Sungkiang residence.

The massive altar table and seats of granite stand beside a private burial ground. Here the members of the family come to offer homage to the memory of their ancestors. Built in the early Sung Dynasty. Near Hangchow.

Pebbles laid in geometric patterns form the paving of this courtyard. An outcropping of rock is utilized to make the step.

This two-hundred-year-old mulberry tree of a rare species is symbolical of filial piety. The Chinese expressed the individuality even in the design of a base for a tree. This one is hewn from granite. Private garden in Sungkiang.

Another mulberry tree. Note the carved marble base of the wall.

The trees of this small enclosure are protected by an open-work tile wall which serves also as a seat. Private garden in West Lake. Built during the Ming Dynasty.

Roof tile is used for a simple but artistic border around the base of a tree.

Another example of roof tile being utilized as a border. Here it provides a base for a tree with flower beds radiating from it.

A granite four-poster protects this ancient tree.

107

The gardener does not always follow geometric designs for his flower beds. Here the roof tile is used in the shape of a vase.

A modern version of an old art is this adaptation of bottles for flower bed margins.

A striking contrast to European planning is this Chinese central courtyard. Instead of grass or marble and a fountain, we find small flower plots with outlines of vases and single geometric figures edged with brick or tile. In between is firmly packed bare earth with an occasional tree. The scene of this courtyard changes with the seasons in the matter of flowers. For example, during the chrysanthemum season, the flower-beds in the courtyard will be filled with the different colored blossoms. Private garden in Sungkiang. Built during the early Ming Dynasty.

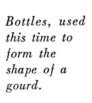

Bottles, used this time to form the shape of a gourd.

Mosaic floors as we know them in Italy, Spain and in South American cities, may well have originated in China, where they were known long before Marco Polo brought back tales of the wonders he found in that flowery kingdom.

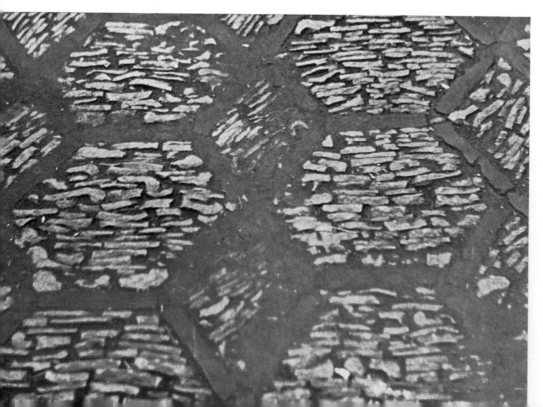

Only gardens of the Ch'ien Lung or earlier periods can boast of such elaborate walks and pavements as illustrated in this group. With small stones of different colors the designer creates the eight symbols of longevity; the emblems of the five blessings; the different shapes of flowers, trees, bamboo and any number of geometrical patterns.

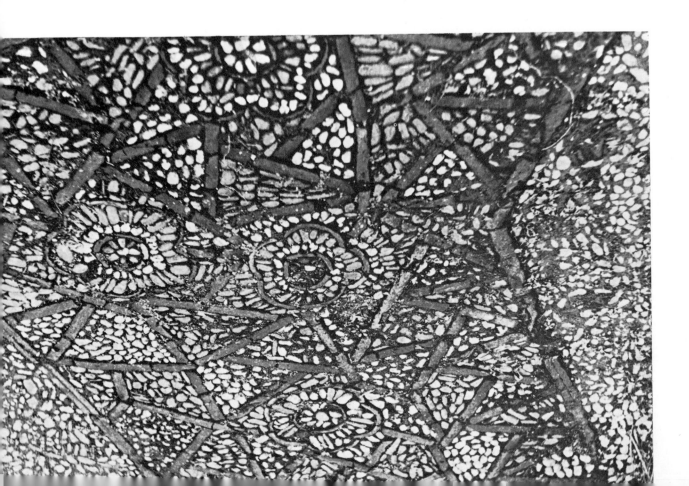

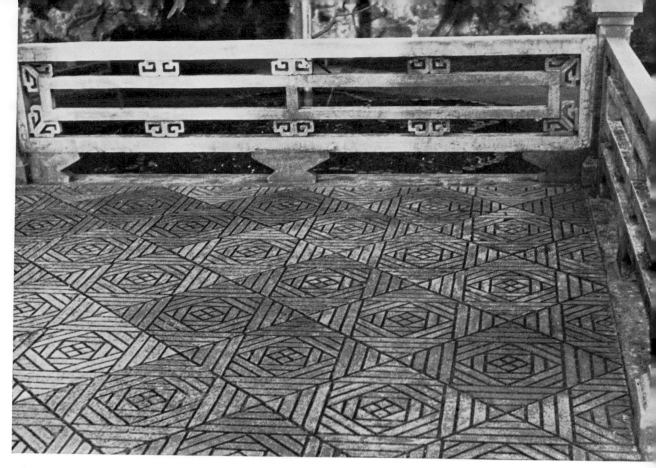

A terrace floor in geometric pattern, with a comparatively plain railing. From a private residence in Hangchow.

From a private garden at Nanking. Built during the early part of the Ming Dynasty, A.D. 1368-1644. Note the growing lotus, the railing of simple design, and the tiles set in the wall.

Wooden railing in a Chinese Temple, Hangchow.
Built during the Ming Dynasty.

Stone railing of very simple and ancient design,
built during the late Yuan Dynasty, A.D. 1126-
1368. Taiping Mountain, near Soochow.

A trellis for roses.

A study of a railing for a modern home. Typical Chinese design of long ago.

Each section individually designed.

Fine example of Chinese carved stone railing with ornamental termination. Len Yin Temple, on the West Lake, Hangchow. Built during the early Ming period.

A stone "prayer-lantern" in front of the Hall of the Eternal Buddha. The characters read: "Praise be to the Eternal One, praise be to Him who is precious, wonderful, victorious and glorious."

These bronze lanterns adorning the Museum of Greater Shanghai are examples of modern Chinese design.

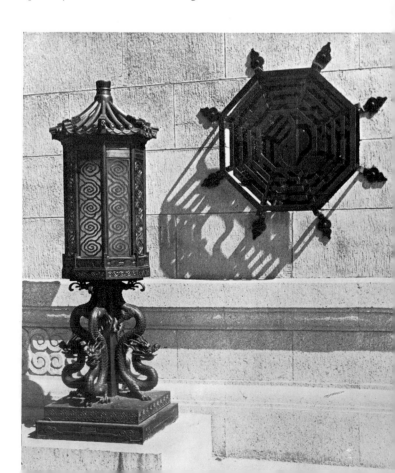

An angular stone bridge in an old Chinese garden at Soochow. Built during the Seventeenth Century.

This granite base for a flag pole is another example of contemporary design.

Note how unobtrusively the Chinese architect has managed to relieve the monotony of this stonework doorway to a Buddhist temple.

This slab symbolizes beauty in the form of the Feng-huang (Phoenix), Imperial Palace, Peiping.

This great slab of snow-white marble is the central section of a stairway leading up to the Imperial Palace in Peiping. It is one of the finest examples of Chinese sculpture. The dominant figures are the two five-clawed dragons, emblematic of imperial power since the reign of Kao Tsu, founder of the Han Dynasty 206 B.C.-A.D. 220. At the bottom are the conventionalized symbols of mountains and seas interspersed with clouds, the symbol of heaven.

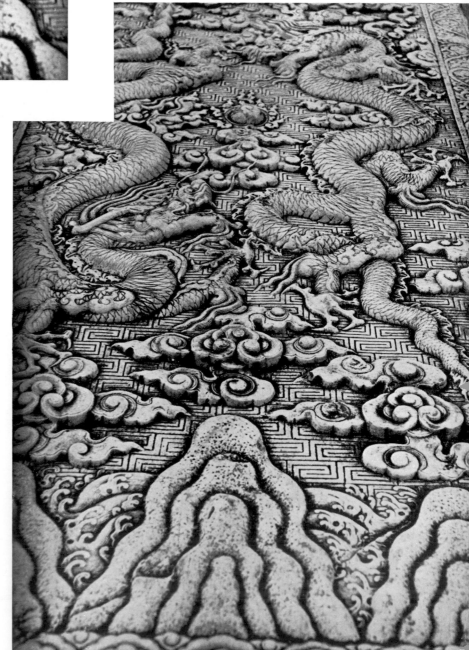

The following designs were drawn from sketches made by the author when it was impractical or even impossible to take photographs.

It is hoped that these designs, aside from their own interest, will prove valuable for their adaptability to the decoration and planning of modern homes. In most instances the drawings represent pure Chinese art, uninfluenced by alien culture. They were sketched directly from originals, the great majority of which were ancient, and are today, alas, forever lost to the world.

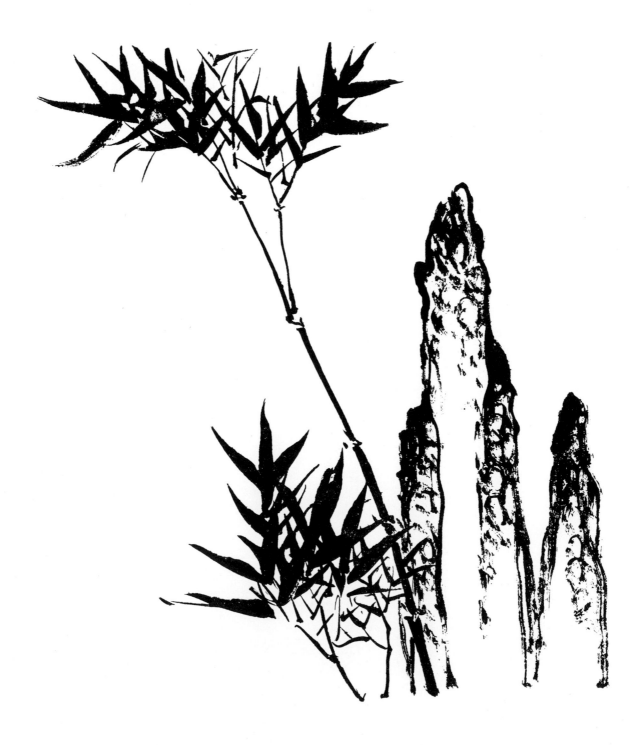

Screen Panels

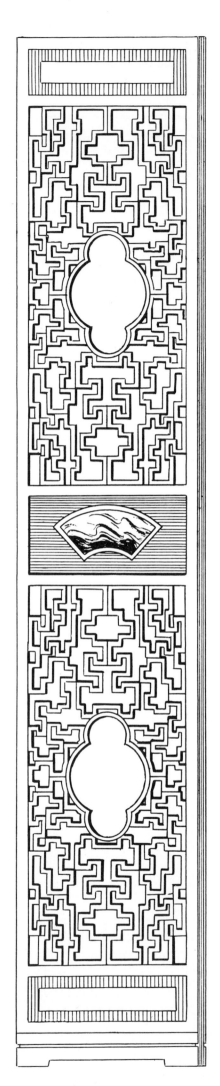
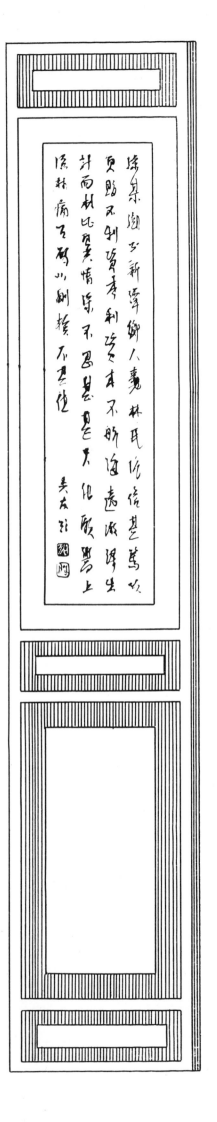

Screen Panels

Screen Panels

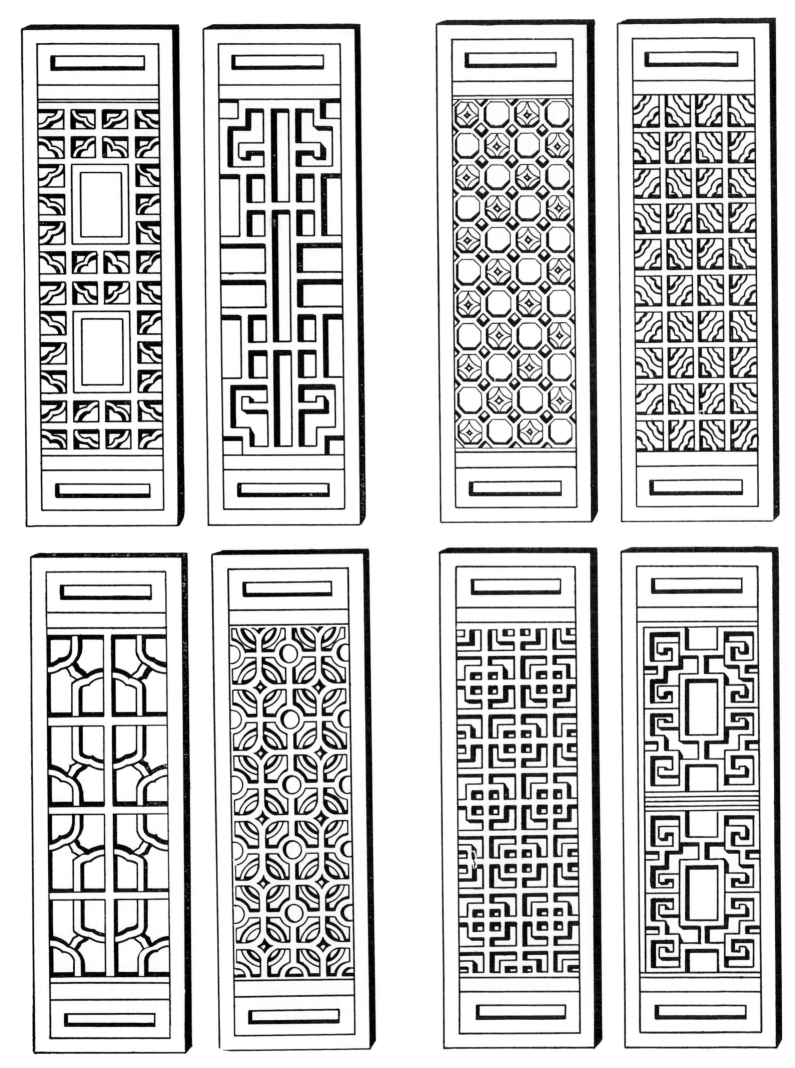

Screen Panels in various patterns.

Carved wood sections of terrace railings.

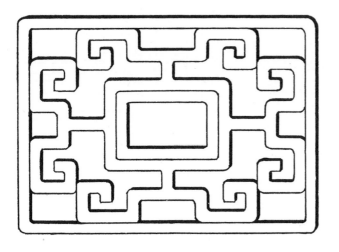

Window grilles of unglazed clay.

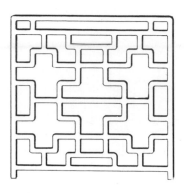

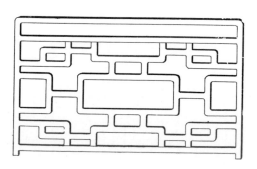

Various grilles of familiar patterns.

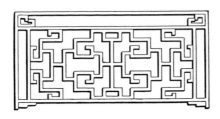

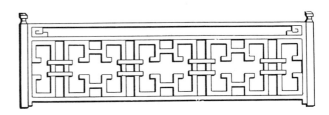

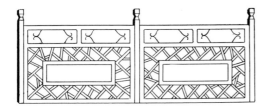

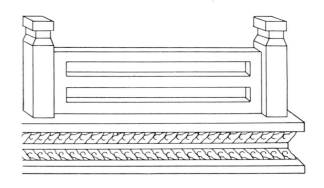

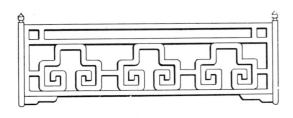

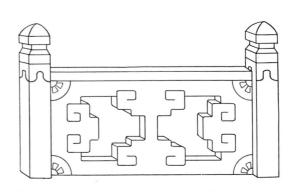

Railings and panels of wood and stone.

Marble or granite railings of characteristic designs.

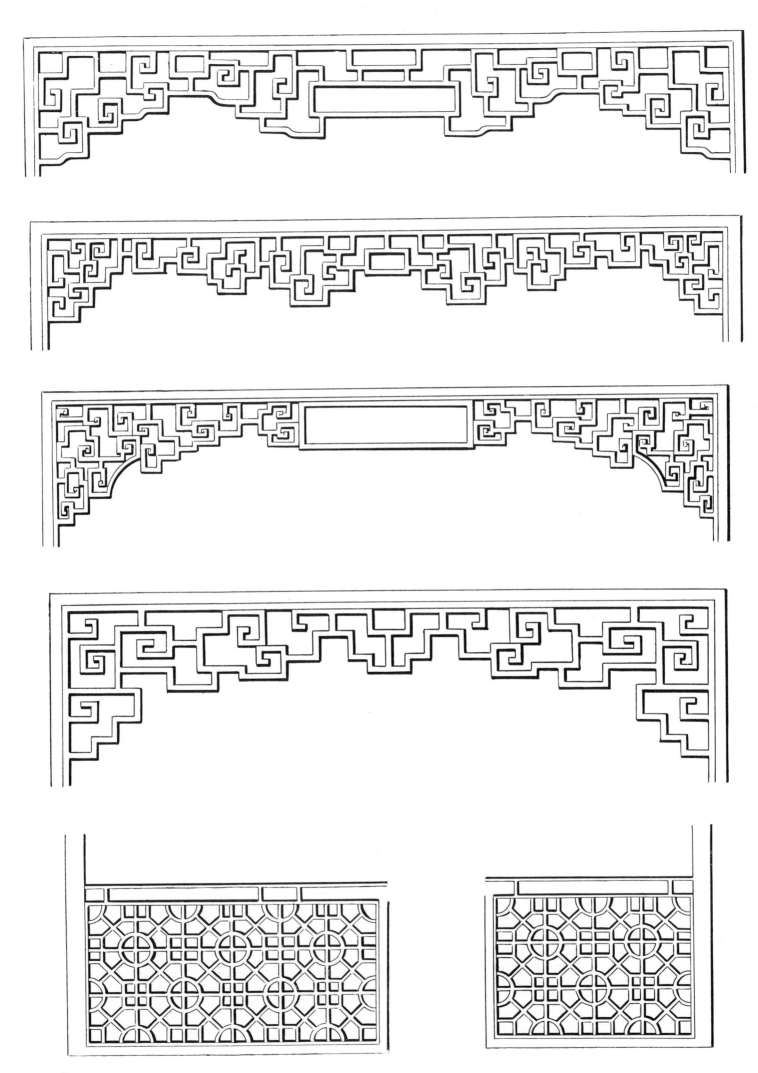

Spandrels and grilles of various patterns.

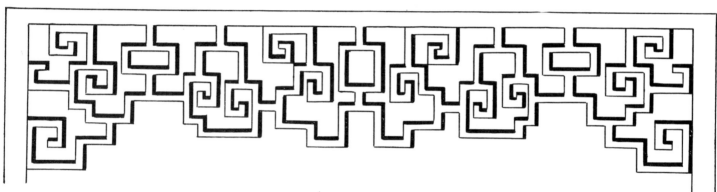

Spandrels of conventional design.

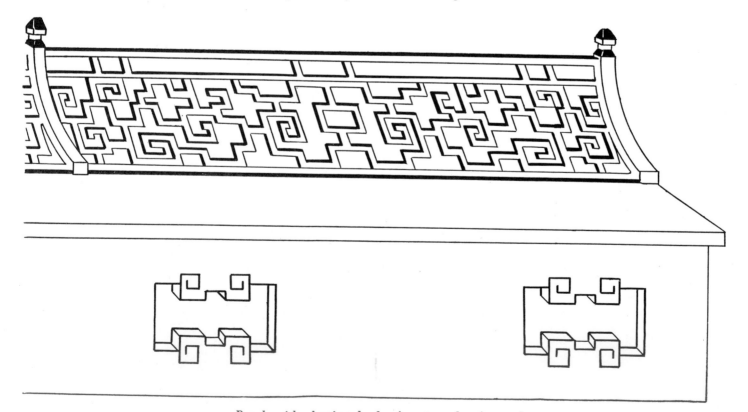

Bench with slanting back of rectangular fretwork.

132

Conventionalized emblems embellish a marble railing.

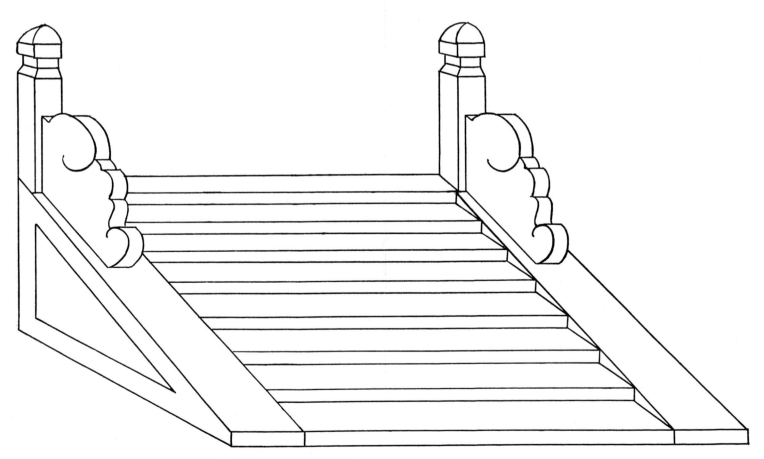

Stair and railing of simple lines.

Woodwork partitions and door decorations elaborately carved.

*Rustic design for railing
and trellis.*

*Casement and door of
bizarre pattern.*

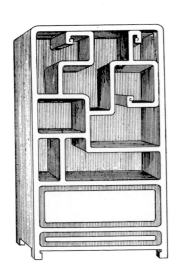

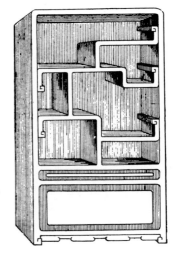

Cabinets with typical complexity of pattern.

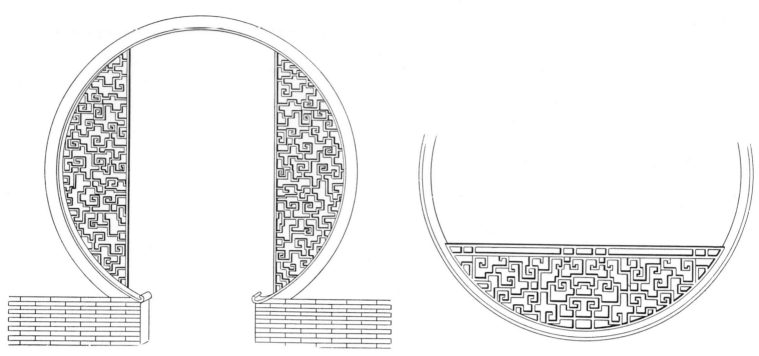

Moon door with rectangular fretwork.

Variation on the carved fretwork.

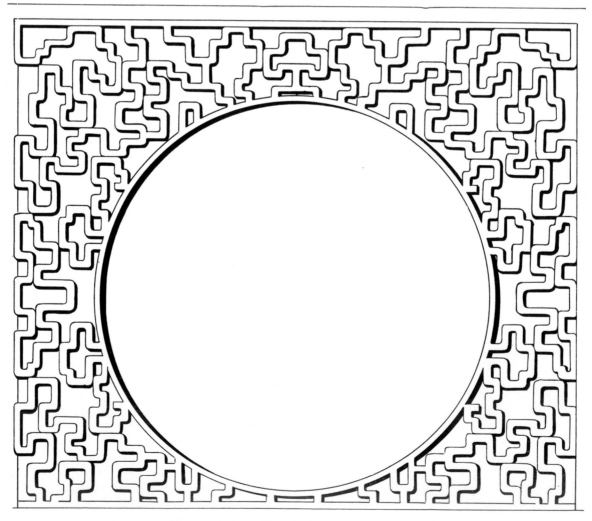

Characteristic grillwork for a circular opening.

Writing desk and tables of old design.

Typical tables of the Ming Dynasty.

138

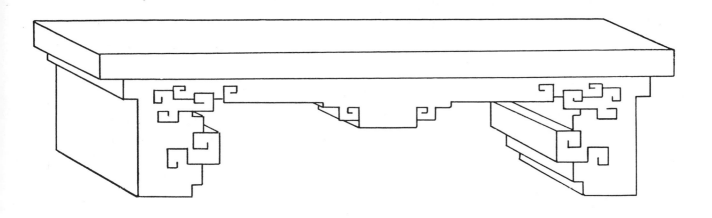

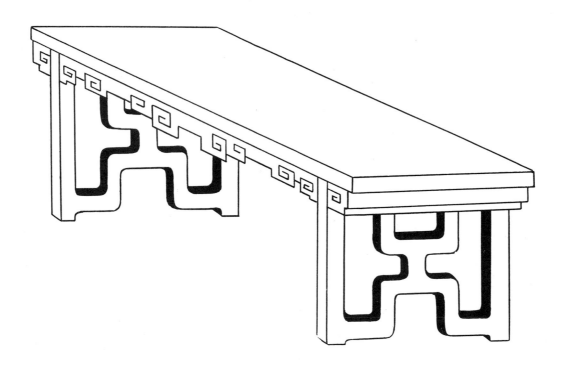

Benches of massive design, ebony, the Chinese t'ieh-li, rubbed to a shiny finish, being a favorite wood.

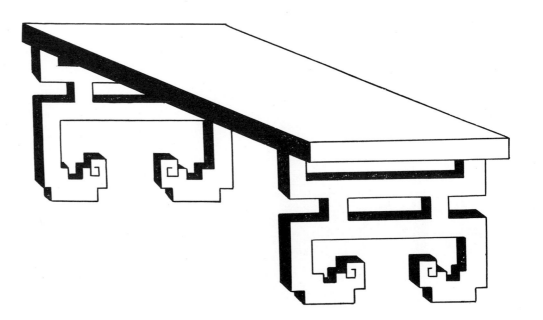

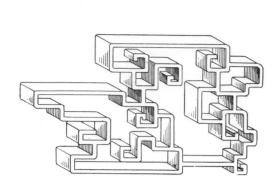
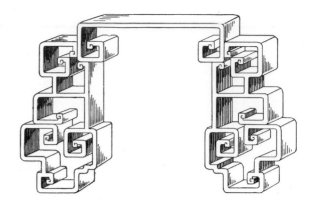

Fanciful tables of complex patterns.

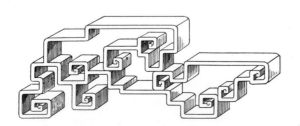
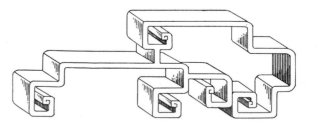

Often rare woods are employed; the dark and heavy tzu-tan is considered most precious.

Chairs Ming Dynasty.

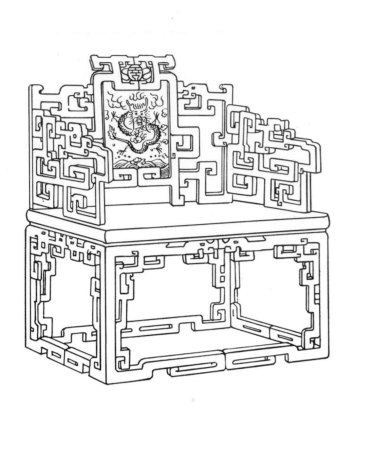

Carved chairs Ch'ing Dynasty (Ch'ien Lung)

142

Flower stands and altar table Ch'ing Dynasty (Ch'ien Lung)

Lacquer chests and table
Ch'ing Dynasty (K'ang Hsi)

Lacquer cabinets Ch'ing Dynasty (Ch'ien Lung)

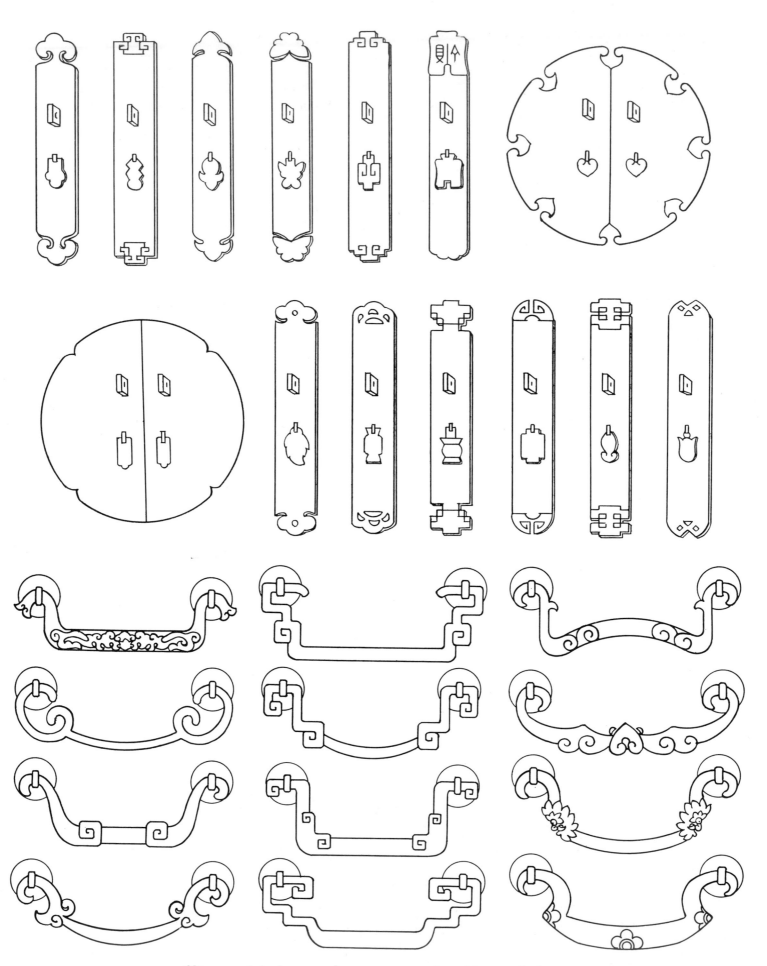

Chinese artistic brass works as ornaments in cabinets and chests.

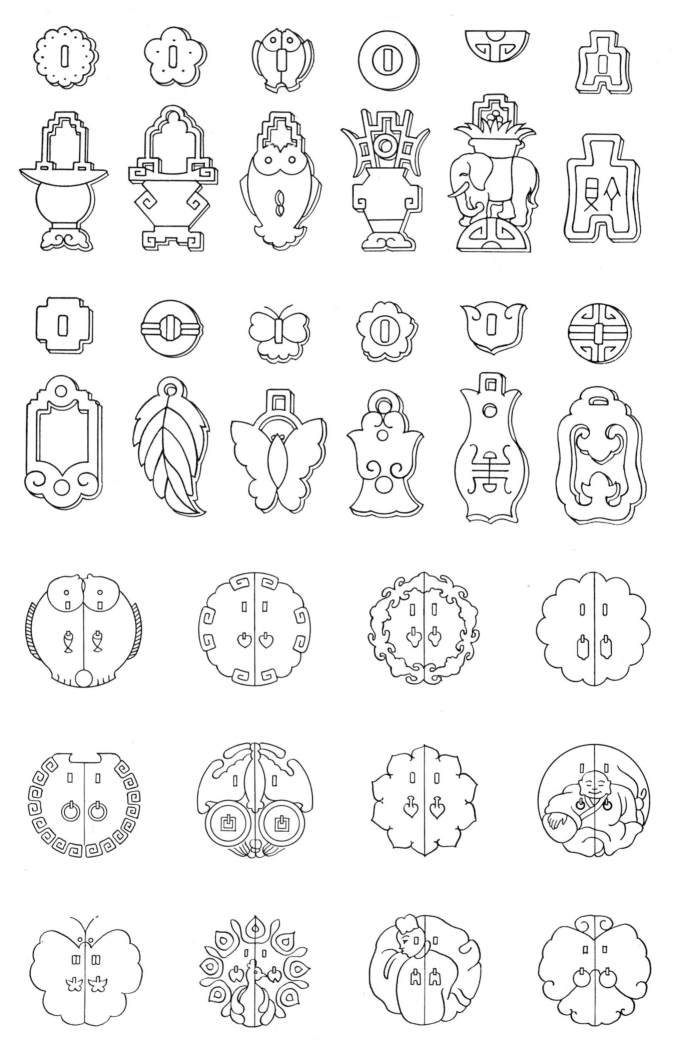

Classical designs in Chinese furniture.

Classical designs in Chinese furniture.